# N̶O B.S.

# GRASSROOTS
# MARKETING

## THE ULTIMATE
## NO HOLDS BARRED
## —TAKE NO PRISONERS—
## GUIDE TO
## GROWING
## SALES AND
## PROFITS OF

## LOCAL
## SMALL
## BUSINESSES

### Dan S. Kennedy & Jeff Slutsky

Entrepreneur.
Press

Publisher: Entrepreneur Press
Cover Design: Andrew Welyczko
Production and Composition: Eliot House Productions

This publication is designed to provide accurate and authoritative information in regard to the subject matter covered. It is sold with the understanding that the publisher is not engaged in rendering legal, accounting or other professional services. If legal advice or other expert assistance is required, the services of a competent professional person should be sought.

**Library of Congress Cataloging-in-Publication Data**
Kennedy, Dan S., 1954–
    No B.S. grassroots marketing/by Dan Kennedy and Jeff Slutsky.
       p.   cm.
    Includes bibliographical references and index.
    ISBN-10: 1-59918-439-7 (alk. paper)
    ISBN-13: 978-1-59918-439-5 (alk. paper)
      1. Marketing. I. Slutsky, Jeff, 1956–. II. Title.
    HF5415.K4515 2012
    658.8—dc23                2011032327

Printed in the United States of America

15  14  13  12                    10 9 8 7 6 5 4 3 2 1

# Contents

PREFACE

**Which Wolves Are Outside Your Door?**

by Dan Kennedy . . . . . . . . . . . . . . . . . . . . . . . . . . . . . ix

CHAPTER 1

**Back to the Future**: What REALLY Works
in Advertising, Marketing, and PR by Jeff Slutsky . . . . . 1

*Branding Gone Wild, 4*
*Traditional Advertising, 5*
*Nontraditional Marketing, 11*
*Selling, 13*
*Advertising Agencies, 14*
*Co-Op Advertising, 15*
*Publicity, 16*
*Conventions, Trade Shows, and Exhibitions, 17*
*Sponsorships, 18*
*Advertising Specialties and Promotional Products, 19*
*My State of This Union's Summary, 19*

CHAPTER 2

**Turning a Problematic Environment
Upheaval to Your Advantage** by Dan Kennedy . . . . .21

CHAPTER 3

**Hard-Nosed, Tough-Minded Investing
in Media and Marketing** by Jeff Slutsky . . . . . . . . . . .27
*Insist on Accountability, 28*
*The Big Picture: Macro ROI, 28*
*What's a New Customer Worth to You?, 31*
*How to Use Tracking Devices with Your*
*Grassroots Marketing Pieces, 37*
*Managing Your Tracking Initiative, 43*
*Managing the Untrackable, 44*

CHAPTER 4

**If You Use Mass Ad Media,
Make Your Ad Dollars Do More** by Jeff Slutsky . . . . . .47
*A Radical Possibility: The Big Cut, 48*
*How to Make TV Deliver More, 49*
*How to Make All Ad Dollars Do More, 50*
*Buy Smarter to Sell More for Less, 55*
*The Bottom Line Is the Bottom Line, 65*

CHAPTER 5

**Taking It to the Streets**: Neighborhood
Marketing Strategies by Jeff Slutsky . . . . . . . . . . . . . .67
*What Is Local-Level Marketing?, 68*
*How Is the Grassroots Marketing Solution Different?, 69*
*Why Local-Level Marketing?, 70*
*Who Implements Local-Level Marketing?, 72*
*The Big McStake, 75*
*The Seven-Step Plan, 75*

*Phase II, 81*

*Turnarounds, 83*

*Maintenance Phase, 84*

CHAPTER 6

**Getting Your Hands Dirty**: Neighborhood
Marketing Tactics by Jeff Slutsky . . . . . . . . . . . . . . . . . .87

*Business Card Handshake, 88*

*Hindsight Promotion, 89*

*The Business Card Drawing, 89*

*Merchant Cross Promotion, 93*

CHAPTER 7

**Rethinking the Business
You Are In** by Dan Kennedy . . . . . . . . . . . . . . . . . . .107

CHAPTER 8

**Inside Your Four Walls** by Jeff Slutsky . . . . . . . . . . . . . .113

*Employee Contest Solutions, 113*

*Customer Referral Program, 115*

*Suggest-Sell Promotions, 117*

*I'll Show You Mine: Reciprocal Displays, 121*

*Internal Signage, 122*

*Your Inside Job, 125*

CHAPTER 9

**The Postman as Your Salesman:** Using
the Most Reliable Small-Business
Marketing Media—Direct Mail by Dan Kennedy . . .129

*Permit Micro-Targeting, 130*

*Facilitate Precise Timing, 132*

*Reach Out to New Movers, 133*

*Reach Out to Known Buyers, 135*

*Switch B2B to Home Addresses, 136*

*Do Follow-Up, 136*

*Marry Direct Mail with All Other Grassroots Marketing, 138*

*Use Direct Mail to Nurture and Maintain*
  *Relationships with Customers, 141*

*The Two Biggest Advantages You CAN Get with Direct Mail, 141*

*The Ultimate Grassroots Direct-Mail Marriage Strategy, 144*

CHAPTER 10

**Fools Rush In**: How to Use—and How to
Waste Dollars on—the Internet and Other
Technology Media by Jeff Slutsky. . . . . . . . . . . . . . .147

*Web Coupons: Be Careful, 147*

*Getting More Visitors to Your Site, 149*

*Sponsored Links: Pay Per Click, 156*

*Your Website, 157*

*Start Marketing Your Website with Free Exposure, 159*

*Constantly Changing, 160*

CHAPTER 11

**The Magical Mystery Bus**: Old and New Marketing
Media Traveling Together by Jeff Slutsky. . . . . . . . . . .161

*Vehicle Advertising, 161*

*Yard Signs, 164*

*Billboards, 166*

*Inflatables and Costumes, 168*

*Email, Voice Mail, Phone, and Fax, 169*

*An Exit Strategy That Helps Bring in Your*
  *Competitor's Orphaned Customers, 172*

*Clever Phone Numbers Help Ring Your Bell, 174*

*Email Is Free Mail, 176*

*Just the Fax, 178*

*Throw Combinations at Them, 179*

CHAPTER 12

**Publicity**: Free Advertising Brought to You
by Your Local News Media by Jeff Slutsky. . . . . . . . .181

*Leverage Your Publicity, 185*
*Easy Ways to Generate Your Publicity, 185*
*Handling a PR Crisis, 187*
*Local PR, 189*

CHAPTER 13

**Come One, Come All to Your Marketing Event**:
How to Get or Multiply Large Numbers
of Customers at Blinding Speed by Dan Kennedy . . .191

*Selling Once to Groups in Events, 192*
*Do's and Don't's of Promotional Events, 195*
*Large Numbers at Blinding Speed, 200*
*When the Circus Came to Town, Everybody Went, 204*

CHAPTER 14

**Profitable Espionage:** Data Mining,
Intelligence Gathering, and Covert
Operations by Jeff Slutsky . . . . . . . . . . . . . . . . . . . . .211

*The Most Profitable, 212*
*Data Mining Your Competition, 218*
*Follow the Leader, 218*
*A Grassroots Mentality, 219*

No B.S. Grassroots Marketing Inconvenient Truths . . .221
Other Books by Dan Kennedy. . . . . . . . . . . . . . . . . .224
Other Books and Videos by Jeff Slutsky . . . . . . . . . .225
Index. . . . . . . . . . . . . . . . . . . . . . . . . . . . . . . . . . . . 229
Free Offer. . . . . . . . . . . . . . . . . . . . . . . . . . . . . . . . .233

# Which Wolves Are
# Outside Your Door?

Dan Kennedy

The recession they claim was over years ago? Big box retailers and discounters? They are losing their war with online discounters—are you? Are you dealing with increasingly fickle customers? Rising costs at every turn? Maybe you have tried mimicking what you see big, national companies do with mass advertising and are finding the effectiveness of traditional media eroding, the promise of new media seductive but then disappointing.

The local small business is a special being. It cannot thrive trying to be a simple, small-size version of big national chains. The strongest, most profitable small businesses are owned and operated and promoted by people who rely predominately on what Jeff calls "grassroots" marketing done at the street level, by direct connection, integrated with the customers, their community, and their daily activities. This has its parallel in politics. Speaker of the House during the Reagan era, Tip O'Neill famously said, "All politics is local." In politics, they say someone is good at "old-fashioned retail politicking," by which they mean organizing volunteers at the local level; getting every door knocked on; getting groups together in people's living rooms for meet-and-greets; getting signs up in lots of yards; having presence at every local festival, fair, high school football game; creating visible association with local officials and celebrities. You might think this is no longer important in today's high-tech age with its proliferate plethora of media, with Facebook and Twitter, with Skype, and so on—but you would be wrong. All of that has become useful, but it has proven unable to replace grassroots work by a grassroots organization as well as candidates themselves.

I occasionally do a little political campaign consulting myself and know some of the big dogs in that field. Recently, an under-30 wunderkind in the field pointed at his magical, mystical phone and said, ruefully, I think resentfully, "Despite everything in here, the guy with the most yard signs and bumper stickers still wins." So, one of my big pieces of advice for local small-business owners, local practice professionals, and local salespeople is the same today as it was 35 years ago when I began giving it: Get up every morning and act as if and organize as if you were running for mayor. It's what Jeff refers to as becoming "mayor" of your local neighborhood or community.

The local small business is a special being. It can easily be eaten by all the wolves at its door if not for a special bond with a sufficient number of customers, clients, or patients who remain immune to seduction by all competitors, who consider themselves to be in a monogamous relationship with their dry cleaner or Main Street store or restaurant, requiring them to be faithful. This presents you with both opportunity for advantage—in creating an asset no big company, big box retailer, or distant discounter can match— and huge hazard, because in many respects this can be the only sustainable advantage available to you, and if you fail at it, you fail entirely. I happen to be a "customers for life" guy. In my own businesses, working indirectly with about a million and directly with about 25,000 small-business owners annually, I call those who discover me and then never leave my "Lifers," and I have many with 7, 10, 15, 20, even 30 years' longevity. In my private marketing consulting copywriting practice, over 85% of all clients repeat, return periodically, and remain in ongoing relationships. Although I admit this next statement is backed by imperfect science, it appears as best we can tell that the small-business owners in over 200 different product and service niches and categories actively using my methodology enjoy substantially higher customer retention, lifetime customer value, and referral value than the averages and norms of their industries. The gist of this, one of my Renegade Millionaire System Principles, is: While most business owners get a customer in order to make a sale, we make a sale to get and keep a customer. This makes the kind of grassroots marketing described in this book all the more important, because the asset at stake is relationship, and that is a very personal, person-to-person thing.

I'll admit, in many ways, the grassroots marketing approach presented here turns the clock back a half a century or more, to a time when advertising was less costly, confusing, and inefficient, when marketing was more direct, when the local merchant and professional had real relationships with their customers. In some ways, many uses of modern media try to simulate this. We advocate returning to it.

I've been in the advertising business my entire life, and, off and on, have worked with some big-name, big corporate clients, but my preference is for aiding the small-business owner with more relationship-based marketing. My co-author, Jeff Slutsky, has perfected what he calls One-On-One Marketing™ as a means of customer connection. Even when he or I work with national franchisors and franchise organizations or chains, we both strive to guide the individual franchise owner or manager to act as if he owned a local business in a small community, and to engage in grassroots marketing at that level—not to rely on brand name or the parent company's big advertising campaigns. Regardless of what kind of business you own, if you'll do the same—if you'll make real grassroots marketing an integral part of your business—you will thrive while others struggle, prosper far more than others in the best of times, and create unique, sustainable advantage.

In this book, we first examine what's wrong with broad-brush uses of traditional and new advertising media and the common mistakes to divorce yourself from. This is important to break free of the ingrained tendencies to "advertise when you need more customers" and to copycat what you see the bigger dogs doing—both hard-to-break habits, both strategically inappropriate and unprofitable for the local small business. Then we proceed with laying out a different approach specifically engineered for the local small business.

Candidly, most marketing books are written very broadly, in hopes that big companies will buy them by the bushel load. This is not such a book. It has been written exclusively for you, the local small-business owner. Unfortunately, a lot of marketing books are written by academics, by big corporate executives, by inexperienced theorists, none of whom have Main Street smarts drawn from actually starting, growing, and running businesses or being on the street, sleeves rolled up, working side by side with business owners. This is not such a book. Its inclusion in my famous *No B.S.* book series is earned precisely because it cites no academics, turns its back on big corporations, brooks no theoretical ideas, nor panders to any reader's hope for "easy buttons" or simplistic solutions to complex problems and opportunities. It is, in fact, no B.S., and consequently, it may not make us a lot of friends in the advertising community, and it may present you with information you'd rather not accept and work you'd rather not have to do. But it will tell you the truth. The unvarnished, unsweetened, unabashed truth.

The local small-business owner is in the fight of his life. Many categories are shrinking by the day: clothing stores, bookstores, gift shops, hardware stores, restaurants, even professional practices, and more. A Darwinian thinning of the herd has been underway in recent years for many reasons: some driven top down from Washington, DC, but others well within the control of the business owner. Business owners lost touch with their customers and communities and forgot all about grassroots activities, and by doing so, left themselves vulnerable to distant and online discounters, big box retailers, and every imaginable kind of competition as well as to recession. Yet, at the same time, in every category, in big cities and small towns, some independent, local small businesses have thrived and grown stronger, have managed to protect their profitability, and have even driven bigger competitors out of their neighborhoods. The strong prosper, so this book is not merely about getting customers, it is about strength.

My co-author Jeff Slutsky is a dedicated champion of small business, at work with such businesspeople, at the grassroots level, day in and day out. He is a smart analyst, ingenious problem solver, a sales expert, and a kindred spirit with me in blunt truth-telling.

I'm proud to welcome him to the *No B.S.* book series, to present his work here, and add a few contributions of my own.

The local small business is not only a special being, it is a noble being. If you are a local small-business owner, entrepreneur, private practice professional, or salesperson, we believe you are engaged in a noble calling.

# CHAPTER 1

# Back to the Future
## What REALLY Works in Advertising, Marketing, and PR

Jeff Slutsky

W e begin with a look at the poor condition of advertising and marketing today, and the problems it presents to the local small-business owner. We face facts. We accurately assess the advertising and marketing landscape. We determine where we are, so that we can get to a better place.

I'm often asked, "What is the best form of advertising?" as if there could be one superior to all others, suggesting that such an answer would solve the business owner's needs, even if it existed. It doesn't and it wouldn't. There is no best. The answer is that nearly every form of advertising can be effective, and every form of advertising can be a total waste of your money. It depends on a number of different factors that are specific to your situation. Those variables include your type of business, your marketplace, your position in the marketplace, your brand equity, the season, your product lines, and so on. It's like asking a doctor which drug is the best. It depends on what the ailment is, what other drugs you're taking, what other conditions you have, your overall health, etc.

What should be asked is, "Which form of *marketing* is best?" Advertising is just one part of marketing. Marketing also includes many other tools like public relations, telemarketing, sales, direct mail, sponsorships, the internet, and a host of others. To continue with the doctor analogy, drugs are just one of the tools at a doctor's disposal. She can also recommend surgery, physical therapy, psychotherapy, nutritional counseling, and exercise or other types of behavior modification. The solutions recommended to a given patient depend on the specific needs of that patient.

Media reps like to play doctor, but have one treatment, regardless of the illness. Unfortunately, after their recommended procedure is over, and in spite of administering a costly remedy, you still suffer from the same ailment.

Most advertising and marketing has become less effective because the consumer has become increasingly immune to it. So, while the advertising media are charging more to deliver messages, those messages are less likely to get noticed and remembered. A study by Yankelovich Partners, an American marketing services consultancy, found that 65% of people now feel "constantly bombarded" by ad messages and that 59% feel that ads have very little relevance to them. Almost 70% said they would be interested in products or services that would help them avoid marketing pitches. Think about that. Seventy percent of consumers will spend money to avoid being bombarded with the never-ending proliferation of marketing messages.

"The Harder Hard Sell," published in the June 24, 2004, issue of *The Economist*, cited a Deutsche Bank report that stated

## NO B.S. GRASSROOTS MARKETING INCONVENIENT TRUTH #1

Advertising is not the only answer to a need for customers or sales. Advertising may not even be the best answer. Advertising relying on out-of-context of marketing fails more often than not. And the least effective advertising, shunned by consumers, is advertising lacking personal relevance to those customers.

Much disappointment, frustration, and failure can be traced to the fool's mission of finding a single, simple solution to a complex problem or opportunity.

–Dan Kennedy

consumers are getting harder to influence due to an invasion of commercial clutter in their lives. The report examined the effectiveness of TV advertising on 23 new and mature brands of packaged goods and concluded that in some cases it was a waste of time and, of course, money. Although in the short term TV advertising would lead to an incremental increase in volume sales in almost every case, there was a positive cash return on that investment in only 18% of cases. Over a longer term the picture improved, with 45% of cases showing a return on investment. The study concluded that "increased levels of marketing spending were less important than having new items on the shelf and increasing distribution."

So what are the reasons that marketing and advertising dollars are rapidly becoming less and less effective? We'll look at two different areas. The first will be the traditional mass media. The second will be a variety of nonmedia-oriented marketing approaches that many businesses attempt to use to increase their overall effectiveness.

## Branding Gone Wild

Before you even begin to consider how to advertise, you need to determine the message you want to share with the consumer. Smaller local and regional businesses have taken a lesson from the major corporations on branding. Yet, when they execute their tactics based on the brand strategy, they often get bogged down in insignificant minutia that doesn't impact the value of the company or drive sales.

There seems to be a lack of common sense when applying corporate brand strategy to the grassroots level. I think the reason is that marketing people generally have pretty healthy egos and they want to make themselves out to be more important or smarter than they really are. We ran up against this, head-on, when working with a client on some very simple promotional tactics that easily would have driven some sales and brought in new customers. It was a franchise company and the marketing director of the franchisor was invited to the meeting where we introduced the various grassroots concepts. The marketing director's biggest concern about the promotion was the typeface that was being used. Fonts are important. But the company had so many other areas where the brand was not being reinforced properly. This type of inconsistency is very common. Even if everything is perfectly consistent right down to the typeface, sorry, but a logo doth not a business make! The small-business owner has to be very careful of copycatting big corporations' obsessions about their brand image, because they are committed to it for many reasons other than impact on sales or importance to customers. The big companies have stockholders' and Wall Street bankers' perceptions and opinions to worry over, concern over franchisees' morale, a need to impose discipline on far-flung operations, and other agendas that you do not have. Yes, brand and image matter, but they can't be permitted to dominate your approach or get in the way of implementing grassroots marketing. And they definitely cannot be seen as the basis for a successful local business.

## Traditional Advertising

### Daily Newspapers

In most markets, the daily newspaper has long been a primary advertising medium for all types and sizes of local businesses. In addition to the major mergers, the increased cost of newsprint, and the downsizing of news staff, the big problems from an advertiser's standpoint are these:

1. Circulation continues to decline annually.
2. Advertising rates increase annually (based on cost-per-subscriber basis).
3. Competition increases from alternative sources for news, sports, business, entertainment, and promotion delivery.
4. An attitude of superiority has developed with an inferior service.

With circulation numbers in the toilet and the remaining readers less likely to pay attention to your ad, you're working with a less efficient medium. Combine that with ever increasing advertising rates, and it's easy to see that local businesses are spending more money to reach dramatically fewer potential customers. Despite this, there are still times when it makes sense to use newspaper advertising. Even then, however, the management at the newspapers acts as if they had the same monopolistic power in the marketplace they once enjoyed several decades earlier. This attitude forces local businesses to seek alternative forms of advertising even after initially considering using the local newspaper.

Use of the newspaper can no longer be an automatic, habitual choice for any business. But it can't be ruled out by a business either. Even though readership quantity has declined and the cost commanded to reach the remaining readership has risen, the issue is one of relevant quality: Who is reading the daily newspaper? Is that reader your ideal client? For example, Dan tells me that free-standing inserts in the local daily newspapers is still one of the top three media used by the nearly 100 seven-figure income-earning leading financial advisors he works with on an ongoing basis, because their avatar clients are 59- to 72-year-old married couples of moderate affluence, retired or nearing retirement, with traditional values. They subscribe to, share, and read the newspaper. On the other hand, auto dealers who still invest an inordinate percentage of their ad budgets in big, full-page, car-and-price newspaper ads hoping to bring the 20- to 40-year-old car, minivan, or SUV buyers are likely to miss a lot more that they could be reaching.

### *Broadcast TV*

Local TV stations have provided a powerful advertising medium to many local businesses over the years. But unlike the daily newspapers, there has been and continues to be some competition between the four major networks and several local independent stations. Just like the daily newspapers, the local TV audiences have been eroding at the same time that spot rates have increased. Broadcast TV has lost audience to cable, satellite TV, video gaming, and the internet. Remote control units and

DVR services like TIVO allow TV viewers to avoid viewing commercials.

Like newspapers, local TV attracts fewer viewers, but charges more, and the viewers that they get are less likely to even see your commercials. Television still has the power to reach a lot of people, but to get any kind of return you'll have to think like a No-B.S. Marketer.

Just as with newspapers, broadcast TV can no longer be an automatic, habitual choice for any business. In both these cases—newspapers and broadcast TV—there are many kinds of local businesses staying there out of habit, or because their direct competitors are there, so they're afraid not to be there with them, or because simply buying space and time is easy. Some are staying put for these reasons and even increasing the amounts spent to get the same results they got a few years before, for less money. This is staying put for all the wrong reasons.

## *Cable TV*

Local cable TV emerged as a great way to supplement a local broadcast TV schedule. For more modest budgets, it was an affordable way to take advantage of sight, sound, and motion in your advertising. At a local level, it could allow you to be on a number of different national TV programs. It was affordable, which allowed you to buy enough frequency to get your message remembered. But, just as cable TV became really valuable as an effective advertising medium, it, too, is being challenged. *Broadcast Engineering* magazine reports that though cable TV remains the predominant technology for the delivery of video programming, cable's share has fallen from almost 100% a decade ago to about 75% of pay-TV subscribers. This is due to competition from direct broadcast satellite TV service, which first became commercially available in 1993. Today, almost 22% subscribe to a satellite service.

## *Radio*

Radio stations have been very good at combining promotional opportunities with their standard airtime programming. Radio is also the most flexible of the mass advertising media. One of the biggest problems with getting results from radio is that there are just too many choices: choosing the right station (usually based on format), at the right day part, with the right number of commercials (frequency), for an effective duration of time (schedule), with the right message (creativity). Then, you have to factor in what other media and marketing approaches you are using along with it (media mix). Plus, there's one element that often gets overlooked, and that's the cost to reach each member of the listening audience. This element is generally expressed as the "cost per thousand" (CPM). In comparing stations, you need to know what you're paying to reach each 1,000 listeners of your target audience. Just because a station is "number one" doesn't mean it's number one for *you*. Too often, the biggest mistake local businesses make with radio is they buy too little too often to really make it work. Even if you figure all that out, you have to come up with a message that gets the job done for you.

One last problem: geography. Many local small businesses using radio reach large numbers of listeners who live and work too far away or migrate to and from work and home by routes that make the advertiser extremely inconvenient to patronize. If the advertiser has a true destination business—like the local zoo or a truly unique and exceptional restaurant—that's one thing; if he has three dry cleaner stores, or a chiropractic clinic serving a cluster of neighborhoods, it's another. Advertisers who deliver services or send sales agents to homes or businesses enjoy a very different dynamic with radio advertising than do retail shops and restaurants. Advertisers who offer goods at their physical location(s) but also via an online store also have a different kind of opportunity with radio advertising than those who must get a customer to their physical location. In the face of all those choices, radio is also suffering from an erosion of its audience. Local radio now competes with satellite radio, audio CDs, DVDs, iPods, cell phones, and GPS. Even with somewhat of a renaissance due to live streaming on the internet, radio can't deliver the audience size it once did.

Bridge Ratings recently did a study to see what effect MP3 players are having on radio listenership among 12- to 18-year-olds. Not surprisingly, people who owned players have tuned in less since the purchase of their MP3 player. They also mention in an earlier study that audiences are listening to a wider variety of music genres, forcing radio stations to change their programming.

Yet radio is perhaps the most affordable of all the major mass media, and it's one of the most flexible as well. So, despite its drawbacks, and because of its virtues, radio is one of the few mass advertising media I tend to recommend to the majority of local business owners as something they need to at least aggressively experiment with. In our seminars, I frequently hear attendees say that they've tried radio and insist it doesn't work for their kind of business, despite proof of continuing use by exactly their kind of business. It is not as simple as writing a commercial and buying time. In fact, because the commercial is so short and so creatively restricted, the commercial itself is less important than the overall advertising strategy and the grassroots marketing the radio advertising supports.

## *Outdoor Advertising*

Due to the increasing restrictions for new billboards by most communities, there is a shrinking amount of good inventory in outdoor advertising. Limited supply means you'll probably pay a premium for it. Even with some of the other outdoor alternatives like wrapped buses, mall posters, phone kiosks, taxi tops, and truck side panels, your message has to be painfully simple to work. For that reason, outdoor advertising is generally better suited to national advertisers with a high degree of existing brand awareness. For local advertisers on a limited budget, it's often too costly and too limiting to get a return. Even the cost of the production (i.e., usually a full-color vinyl covering) can cost as much as a month of exposure.

### Yellow Pages Directories

It's not uncommon for a small business to devote half of its advertising budget to Yellow Pages advertising. This used to be a must-buy for any type of local, community, or neighborhood service company. When there was a problem, your furnace was broken, your toilet was backed up, or you had to get your grease trap cleaned at your restaurant, you usually let your fingers do the walking. But this approach has changed with the proliferation of directories and web-based or cell-based alternatives including services like Angie's List, Yelp, Craig's List, Four Square, and specialized mobile apps.

## NO B.S. GRASSROOTS MARKETING INCONVENIENT TRUTH #2

It doesn't make sense to promote your Yellow Pages ad in your other advertising. Why would you direct a potential customer to the only medium that puts you directly next to all of your competitors?

Yellow Pages advertising was always expensive, but often a necessary evil. Plus, their sales forces often approached your business like storm troopers, using scare tactics to get you to buy, and buy big. And once you made a decision, you were stuck with it for an entire year.

### *Weeklies, Tabloids, and Other Miscellaneous Print Advertising*

Many options exist: local magazines and suburban newspapers; specialty publications and penny savers; and bowling sheets and church or school bulletins and event programs. These options are not really what I would consider major mass media, but they are often part of the media mix. In reality, this type of advertising is the proverbial black hole of marketing. It sucks up a lot of marketing dollars and what is returned is often a mystery.

My co-author, Dan Kennedy, cautions business owners about too quickly abandoning this "old media," though, especially for emergency-response kinds of businesses and/or when aiming at consumers age 50 and up, and certainly 60 and up.

## Nontraditional Marketing

Now that we've looked at the traditional advertising media, the next area that needs to be explored covers the nontraditional forms of marketing that can eat up huge chunks of your budget.

### *Internet*

The internet is sexy, exciting, explosively growing, and for most, necessary, but can still cause you to waste tens of thousands of dollars. The proliferation of online marketing media is so new and so subject to constant rapid change that the rules and the metrics are being rewritten on a weekly basis. A grassroots marketing solution will almost certainly include some use of the internet. The key is balancing your greatest possible return against your investment in both time and money.

There are many different ways of sinking your marketing dollars down this electronic well. A really good functional website can end up costing a small fortune to develop. Once you get it started, it often takes on a life of its own. It requires more and more updating and maintenance. Every little change and improvement costs more money.

Other marketing avenues include spam, pop-ups, banner ads, blogs, e-commerce, and e-zines. Just as new avenues for sending advertising messages via the internet open up, companies develop software to block those messages. There are sponsored links on Google, MSN, Yahoo!, and other search engines or browsers where you "pay-per-click" (PPC). There are unique URLs and other sites to help you promote and sell, including eBay, Amazon, and Overstock. As a No-B.S. Marketer, you will learn which of these online approaches makes the most sense for you.

### *Telephone Marketing and Telemarketing*

This once powerful tool has been significantly dulled with new laws. Do-not-call lists, caller I.D., blocked calls, and cell phones that create less reliance on land lines have sent this marketing powerhouse into the outhouse. Yet there are still opportunities. Regardless of the difficulties, some form of telephone marketing is usually an efficient way of beefing up your marketing.

Local companies usually don't think about the inbound element of telephone marketing. You can spend money on all of these marketing programs to motivate a customer to call you, but if the fielding of that inbound inquiry is unprofessional, you can lose those potential customers (even with the advertising doing what it's supposed to do). Answering machines, voice mail, automated call attendants, and interactive voice response

(IVR) systems are just as frustrating as talking to an inept, under-trained, disinterested receptionist.

A No-B.S. Marketer knows that you have one shot at a potential customer when that person calls your business. This point of first contact is critical, yet it is often the weakest link in the marketing chain for most businesses, large and small.

## Selling

Selling and marketing don't get along. The sales force and the marketing staff are usually at odds in many organizations. A No-B.S. Marketer, however, views the sales staff as one more marketing tool. A No-B.S. Marketer also recognizes that in smaller companies there may not be a person with the title of "salesperson." But there are people in nearly every business that must do some kind of selling as part of their responsibilities. The selling function is oftentimes the final step in the marketing process of getting that customer to buy for the first time. Asking for the order can be as elaborate as getting the final paperwork that closes the deal on a dozen jumbo jets, or it could be as simple as, "Would you like fries with that?" It's all selling.

Consider this example: Many years ago, while working for a small advertising agency, I convinced my father to let me do a small direct-mail campaign to promote the family's office coffee service. I created a direct-mail campaign with a series of mailers. The photography, design, layout, and printing were done on trade for coffee, so that there was little out-of-pocket cost except for the mailing list and postage. I then used some eye-catching headlines including: "My Coffee Is Worth Beans" and "Use My Bunns™ Free" (Bunn was the brand name of the coffee maker my father used).

The mailers generated several inbound inquiries. One was from a major mortgage company that used 16 boxes of coffee a month. My father's largest customers at that time only used five boxes of coffee a month. This campaign had created a lead of significant size. My father made the phone calls, answered some questions, and gave some prices, but he never followed up. He wasn't a salesman. They never called back, so the opportunity just faded away. Did the advertising work? It did in the sense that it generated a good lead. However, an overall marketing campaign, which must include a sales effort and a follow-up, wasn't implemented at all. Consequently, the total program failed. The bottom line is that the integrated marketing program did not end up providing a return on the marketing investment (even though the investment was very small in real dollars).

Now consider an example from an industry that focuses on their salesmen: Jeannie, our office manager, went shopping for a midsized four-door sedan. She told each salesman that with only two kids it was important to her to have a car that seated six people, but she did not want a minivan. Five of the six salesmen kept trying to sell her a minivan. "They wouldn't listen to me." she says. "I told them I did NOT want a minivan, but as soon as they found out I was a mother of two, they kept pitching me the minivan." The dealership that ultimately got the sale was the one where the salesman listened to what she wanted and never mentioned anything about a minivan.

## Advertising Agencies

Ad agencies deal with both the media and the creation of the message. They usually like to think of themselves as full-service marketing companies. The message of your marketing is just as important as the delivery of that message. You'll spend a certain amount of money getting that message out to your potential buyers. That investment can generate many new customers or none, depending on how effective the message was.

The problem with small local advertising agencies is that most of them dream of being large national advertising agencies. It's a creative business, but sometimes the creativity gets in the way of the selling message.

### *The Message Must Reflect Reality*

One other problem is that an agency can come up with a wonderful slogan, but that doesn't mean that what happens at the point of sale reflects the message sent. I've been to a Radio Shack and got *no answers* to my questions. I've been to a McDonald's where they could care less if I smiled.

From the agency, to their corporate client, to the point of the final sale, the message has to be consistent and accurate. Just because something is presented in advertising doesn't make it true in the real world, which is why there is a distrust of advertising.

As a subset to advertising agencies, there are all those vendors that market their unique services. These include production houses, animators, jingle writers and producers, photographers, graphic artists, copy writers, and so on. Each pushes his own service. The account executive working for a jingle company is selling jingles. Do you need a jingle? Could the jingle money be used more effectively elsewhere?

The same goes for your logo. Most logos used by local businesses don't make any sense. I've seen hundreds of random designs that have no meaning. The business owners are proud of their logos. Nonetheless, like any other form of marketing, a logo has to do a job. It has to help sell.

## Co-Op Advertising

Free money is being wasted. It's yours for the taking. Companies that offer co-op advertising plans for their products cover the retail spectrum from cars to computers to cosmetics. There is $50 billion available in co-op funds, plus over one thousand manufacturer programs that reimburse 100% of your qualified advertising expenditures according to the *Co-op Advertising Programs Sourcebook*™. But according to the Yellow Pages Publishers Association (YPPA), a significant amount of this money goes unused. Many retailers fail to use available funds because they are unaware of them or believe that qualifying for them would be too difficult.

## Publicity

The most common misconception is that it's free. It's not. It is true that there is no cost paid to media for the placement of a message, but there are other costs to create news releases and collateral material, and time is needed to pitch the story to the press. Having said that, publicity can provide great value compared to traditional advertising. The downside is that you have no control over the message. In spite of its advantages, publicity is an overlooked opportunity for many local businesses. Time is the issue. You don't have the time or know-how to suggest a newsworthy story to the press, and the opportunity is lost. You can hire a PR firm to do it for you, and more times than not, you won't get your ROI. The news media is besieged by countless requests, and on a local level, you have a finite number of decent press outlets for your stories.

The biggest advantage of getting a story is that it is more credible than advertising. The news is the very reason people read publications, and watch or listen to the news. If you can become part of the news, you potentially make a big impact. But reporters are not interested in providing your business with free advertising. No-B.S. Marketers know how to present their story idea so that a reporter will be interested. No-B.S. Marketers also work publicity into their overall marketing programs. And this integration provides leverage that yields an impressive multiple return on your invested marketing dollars.

## Conventions, Trade Shows, and Exhibitions

These events are a major expense for many companies because they involve all the different types of corporate communications. The most involved is the annual convention. Generally, once a year, a company will bring in their front line people. That could be their franchisees, store managers, dealers, and agents, along with vendors and the corporate support people. It is an opportunity to introduce new ideas, procedures, products, and services. It also is used to fire up the troops and help different groups network. With the massive cost of one of these events, it is critical that companies and organizations demand a much higher return on their investment. This includes boring industry speakers. They may be able to present the right information, but if the audience is asleep, are you really getting your ROI for having your attendees in that breakout session?

As a grassroots marketer, you will need to plan each event from beginning to end so that the business will get maximum results for the least amount of money. You can still offer maximum entertainment value and at the same time reinforce your critical messages.

### *Consumer Shows*

Local businesses spend a lot of money participating in these specialty shows. They may include car shows, home shows, lawn and garden shows, boat shows, and so on. In theory, they're a great way to get many would-be buyers to come see your booth and learn about your products and services. But what is the return? First, you have to look at all the expenses connected to

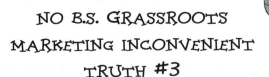

## NO B.S. GRASSROOTS MARKETING INCONVENIENT TRUTH #3

More marketing dollars are wasted on local sponsorships than just about anything else. Unless you know how to leverage a sponsorship, you'll probably see no return on your investment. So unless your kid is on the team, don't waste your money.

participating in the show. The booth fee is just a small part of it. If you want electricity, you have to pay a union person to plug in your cord. Then, there's the cost of moving all your stuff there, the cost to staff the booth, and the cost to have a compelling, eye-catching display and giveaways at your booth.

Now, in spite of all the time and expenses of participating in a show, most participants have no strategy for turning the thousands of lookers into buyers. Of course, some will have a free drawing so they can generate a database with the information they collect, but, all too often, they don't convert that effort into sales.

### Sponsorships

A lot of money is spent on local sponsorships. It could be for sporting events or fundraisers. There's usually some media exposure and logos are displayed—plus my favorite, the T-shirt with 27 tiny logos all over it. Most sponsorship money is a total waste. Often, because it supports a local worthy cause, the ROI is not held to the same standards as traditional advertising. Perhaps this is because the money comes out of a different budget. As a No-B.S. Marketer, you need to examine each potential sponsorship opportunity and structure the arrangement so that you can maximize the return. If you're not getting buying customers from your involvement with a sponsorship, your money should be put elsewhere.

## Advertising Specialties and Promotional Products

According to the Professional Products Association International, promotional products make up a $17.3 billion industry. That's a lot of tchotchkes. These items can be anything that can carry a logo or slogan, from caps to cups, keepsakes, coasters, clocks, combs, clips, chairs, and a million other types of crap. Yes, they can help customers remember your business name or give you something to talk about at your trade show or sales call. But unless you incorporate your giveaways and getaways into your overall grassroots marketing strategy, they're just so much trinkets, toys, and trash. For most small businesses, it may only cost a few hundred here and there. It adds up and, if not used effectively, squanders valuable resources that could be more readily used to bring customers through the front door.

## My State of This Union's Summary

These are some major problems with marketing, and they're going to get worse. In the near future, the traditional advertising media will become less cost effective for most average businesses. The nontraditional marketing approaches will become increasingly difficult to adapt and manage. You'll be besieged by throngs of salespeople touting stats that prove their station, publication, or cyber stuff will bring you business. To make your marketing and advertising money work smarter, you'll need to re-evaluate ALL of your marketing. Though it's impossible to start with a clean slate, you can start with a fresh focus called "zero-based marketing." Look for alternatives and supplements in places you never thought of before. You'll need to examine different and unique approaches to marketing that all work synergistically together while seamlessly functioning within your operation. Now that you see most of the problems, you can start working on your No-B.S. Marketer strategies, plans, tactics, and *solutions*.

Zero-based marketing might also be called "clean-slate" or "start anew marketing." It means setting aside all preconceived notions, all personal likes and preferences, all existent methods, all habits, every "but this is the way we've always done it," and taking an entirely fresh look at what works best and can deliver the best customers at the best cost, in your particular situation. This may very well mean going back to the future, to focus on very unsexy grassroots opportunities and methods, and giving them greater priority than the newest, most talked about, most hyped media. It may very well mean going back to basics of direct customer contact, effective salesmanship, and quality relationships. It means approaching the entirety of this book with no biases for your present methods, no biases against any method. Everything is on the table.

# CHAPTER 2

# Turning a Problematic
## Environment Upheaval
## to Your Advantage

Dan Kennedy

I like to listen to old radio programs on CDs, on the rare occasions I have to drive any significant distance. Many of these CDs have the original commercials intact. In a series of Phillip Marlowe detective dramas—based on the character created by the legendary writer Raymond Chandler—there are commercials for the 1950 Ford sedans, and they are really spectacular radio commercials. They feature true Unique Selling Propositions: Ford had the only budget-priced sedan with a powerful V-8 versus all others in their class with 6-cylinder engines; they had "king-size brakes" typically found only in much more expensive cars, providing maximum safety; and so on. Some of the commercials featured testimonials, like an airline pilot comparing the experience of driving this car to that of flying a plane, soaring above the crowds. They all had a strong call to action, pushing listeners to immediately arrange a test drive. And they all directed listeners where to find their local dealer in their phone directories, plus this line: "*. . . or perhaps you know him personally.* He'll be happy to arrange . . ." The idea that you might know your local Ford dealer personally, whether you do or not, is a powerful piece of persuasion. It suggests that your Ford dealer is a man of your community, a neighbor, a person who is accessible to you, out and about, there to be held accountable. And even if you don't actually know him personally, it reminds you that it feels like you do, because he appears in his own advertisements with his family and pets, and you know things about him as a result of his advertising, marketing, and public relations, maybe, that he was a war hero or a star on the area's college sports team or spearheads a big fundraising effort each year for the volunteer fire department.

This idea of personally knowing the people we do business with may seem to have gone by the wayside given all the broadcast marketing offline and on, all the commerce done at distance, all the automation, and the prevalence of the giant

---

### NO B.S. GRASSROOTS MARKETING INCONVENIENT TRUTH #4

There is no substitute for REAL, personal, person-to-person relationships.

---

chains. As an example of the dominance of giants, over 60% of consumers involved in home improvement projects in 2010-2011 cited purchasing from Home Depot, Lowes, and Walmart, while only 3% cited purchasing from independent retailers. So you may think the actual or at least felt personal relationship an unnecessary antique of a bygone era, memorialized only in old black-and-white TV shows about small-town life. To the contrary, one of the few advantages the small, local merchant, service provider, professional, or sales professional can own in the war with the giants and discounters is this kind of personal relationship, or at least sense of personal relationship, to be enhanced with No B.S. Grassroots Marketing.

Please disabuse yourself of the idea that people no longer want this. Ninety percent of college students physically visited their local bank branch at least once a month in 2010, despite being able to do all banking online, from their wizard phones. Some people may not realize how much they want it unless and until they get it, but almost everybody prefers dealing with people rather than faceless institutions, prefers human contact and interaction to distance and isolation, welcomes a warm smile and a kind word from someone who knows them by name and asks how their cat is doing. Further, most people like feeling that they know the people they are doing business with. I have proven beyond any shadow of a doubt that financial advisors', chiropractors', dentists', and in- home service providers' "closing percentages" (conversion of prospects to clients, patients, and customers), average transaction sizes, and referrals go up almost in direct proportion to the extent of personal disclosure done by the seller. In short, the more the prospects know about the person they are contemplating buying from, the more likely they are to buy. For this reason, in most of the advertising I develop as one of the highest-paid direct response copywriters in the country, for clients in hundreds of different fields, I include personal stories and seemingly unimportant details about the person behind the advertised company or product.

How does all this relate to the "state of the union report" Jeff gave in Chapter 1, about your advertising and marketing media choices?

First, I am a champion of the idea that there is neither good nor bad media per se, just as neither hammer nor scalpel nor gun is a good or bad tool. It depends on the purpose it is to serve and the capability of the person using it. The merits of any and every advertising and marketing tool, media, strategy, or tactic are totally situational.

Second, the merits of one almost always depend on the context of use and synergy with others. A billboard-wrapped truck in and of itself may have very limited value, as Jeff mentioned, largely due to the painfully brief message that can be grasped at 55 miles per hour (and realistically, who drives 55 mph anymore?). But if that billboard-wrapped truck is strategically parked in a neighborhood where work is being done on a happy customer's home, from 5:00 to 6:30 P.M., when all the neighbors are returning home from work AND the people working on the house are in good uniforms and, if approached, are able and eager to answer questions and collect information or immediately whip out a cell phone and connect the prospect with a salesperson back at the office AND the surrounding homes get a multistep mailing campaign immediately after the work on Herb and Betty's house is done, beginning with a testimonial letter from Herb and Betty to their neighbors, well, the billboard-wrapped truck may be very valuable indeed.

Third, and most important—MOST important—when advertising and marketing media are used in a way that makes the connection human, from a person to another person, and reminds that "he is my local Ford dealer I probably know personally"— used in a "grassroots" way—it is all infinitely more effective.

Jeff has fairly and accurately assessed the facts of life of advertising and advertising media. The audience is fragmented; the media and the messages are increasingly ineffective; the costs are climbing even as the reach, readership, audience, and attention given is declining; and the need to be present in more media and more places is very challenging to the business owner with limited resources, who already feels stretched too thin. If you want to view all this as adversity, then be reminded of one of the key principles presented in Napoleon Hill's seminal work, *Think and Grow Rich*: In every adversity lies the seed of equal or greater opportunity. There is opportunity here to be had, advantage to be taken: It is being person-to person and personal in an ever more impersonal marketplace. It is in *the way you use* whatever media you use, not just in choices of media or in hopeful search for the "magic pill" newest media.

The No-B.S. Marketer is and must be ruthless in holding advertising and marketing and sales media, investments, and activities financially accountable, as Jeff emphasizes in his next chapter, and I expound on in my book *No B.S Ruthless Management of People and Profits*. The No-B.S. Marketer must be a militant pragmatist, wary of the kind of creativity for creativity's sake Jeff mentioned ad agencies are often guilty of, and wary of whatever next, new, bright, shiny object is waved in front of him.

But he must also be creative in ways that create that sense of person-to-person, personal relationship. He must use media as an extension of personality and relationship, not as a substitute for it. This is where advantage is to be found, at the grassroots level. The giants have no alternative but to use media as substitute for relationship. The most successful local small-business operators will do exactly the opposite.

# CHAPTER 3

# Hard-Nosed, Tough-Minded
## Investing in Media and Marketing

Jeff Slutsky

What is a successful marketing program? Most businesspeople would probably tell you it's one that generates new customers or increased sales. But how do you know if your marketing program is doing its job? Figuring that out is tougher. The key measurements of your marketing program must include tangible benefits such as revenue or profit or customer activity. It's not enough to justify it with cost efficiencies in media buying or subjective "measurement" of creative programs.

The first step in developing your grassroots marketing program is to determine what your desired result is in any or all given marketing components, as well as for your overall marketing program. To do that, all of your marketing initiatives must have some tracking capabilities. You will also need to be able to calculate how much you're willing to invest to generate a new customer or expand your sales from an existing customer. Doing so helps you calculate your return on marketing dollars or budget invested.

## Insist on Accountability

Your marketing results must be measurable to be practical. Without measurability, there's no accountability. Without accountability, you can't calculate your ROI (return on investment). And without calculating your ROI, you can't determine if you're getting your money's worth. Therefore you need to have the means to determine if all of your various forms of marketing are getting the desired results. If you can't incorporate a tracking procedure that allows you to measure the results of your marketing, you're at risk of wasting money, time, and opportunity.

## The Big Picture: Macro ROI

No, it's not an imitation Italian dish made with pasta and cheese. It's a big picture view of your marketing's effectiveness and a good place to start learning how to generate a good return on your marketing investment.

Add up all the expenditures directly related to your marketing. Include all traditional advertising, plus community involvement programs like church bulletins, high school newspapers, Little League sponsorships, and Main Street festivals. If you've purchased any specialty items with your logo on them like pens, T-shirts, coffee cups, key chains, refrigerator magnets, and so on, put them in the pot. If you have provided in-kind support, include your cost of donating the product or service. Don't forget your Yellow Pages ads, message on hold, internal telemarketers, salespeople, giveaways like tickets to concerts, or lunches with prospects. Oh! And don't forget your basic marketing billboard promotional piece: your business cards.

Add any design work like logo development and website design. Also assign an appropriate amount for items you use for multiple purposes including marketing (e.g., stationery) and add that amount to your marketing costs. Once you add up the price of all the items, you will have an accurate idea of your marketing costs. Compare it against your total gross and net sales.

Now, what would happen if you could get the same level of sales and cut your marketing budget in half? A No B.S. Grassroots Marketing Solution may help you do just that. But you will have to make some tough choices and difficult changes.

### Calculating Your ROI

In his book *Return on Marketing Investment*, Guy R. Powell defines ROI as "revenue (or margin) generated by a marketing program divided by the cost of the program at a given risk level." This definition works fine for big companies with major budgets. However, since the focus of this book is marketing at the No-B.S. Marketer level, the ROI definition we use is simply "revenue generated by a marketing program divided by the cost of that program." The No-B.S. Marketer definition allows you to express your ROI as a specific dollar amount or as a percentage.

Powell also factors in another element that he calls the "hurdle rate," which he defines as the minimum acceptable expected return of a marketing program at a given level of risk. You don't need to take into account the hurdle rate when following the No B.S. Grassroots Marketing Solution. For most marketing programs executed on the local level, you simply need to know how much revenue you generated in relation to what it cost you to generate it.

The No-B.S. Marketer way uses the same method you would to evaluate a return on any investment, on marketing, or a new delivery van, or a third store. The investment costs you X. That investment generates Y, which is sales, profit, new customers, or whatever other criteria you use to measure company performance. You subtract X from Y, and the result is your ROI. You can express it in real dollars or as a percentage, depending on your objectives.

Consider this example: A radio schedule costs you $5,000. You are promoting a specific product at a specific price that is not being advertised or marketed anywhere else. Consequently, customers who request that deal are most likely to be responding to the radio advertising. There is $10,000 worth of sales for that product. Half of the customers who came to buy that product also bought additional items worth another $3,000 in sales. Your immediate return on gross sales is $13,000 less $5,000, or $8,000 (simple enough to figure out for the radio investment).

But you should also factor in the direct cost of the goods sold. If your margin was an average of 50%, the gross profit generated from this particular radio schedule would be $6,500. The return, therefore, would be $6,500 minus $5,000, or $1,500. You could say either that the advertising was profitable or that there was a 30% return.

There are other considerations when calculating ROI. For example, of those customers who bought as a result of that radio schedule, how many of them are first-time buyers with your business? If a total of 100 customers spent $13,000 and 25 of them are new customers, you have to look at a few other numbers to determine the ROI:

1. Of the 75 regular customers, how many of them would have purchased that item had you promoted it with less expensive marketing such as counter displays, targeted postcard mailers to customers, or statement stuffers?

2. Did you offer a discount or added value? If so, determine how many of the regular customers would have paid full price if there hadn't been a promotion.
3. Track how many of the 25 new customers return again and become your regular customers. If you were able to determine that of the 25 new customers, 15 of them become regulars, your ROI for that particular radio schedule would be much higher. To figure exactly how much higher, though, you would have to know what a new customer is worth to your business.

## What's a New Customer Worth to You?

It's strange, but many small-business people have no idea what a good regular customer is worth to their businesses. By calculating that, you should gain a better idea of what you're willing to invest or risk to attract a good, regular customer. It also tells you how important it is to keep your existing customers happy. The cost of retaining a customer and even expanding a customer's value is much less then getting a new customer.

To determine what you're willing to invest in marketing, first discover what an average new customer is worth to you. To determine their value, answer the following questions:

1. What is your average sale (transaction amount)?
2. What is the frequency of your average customer? This calculation can be expressed in transactions or visits per week, month, or year depending on the type of operation you run.
3. What percentage of new customers become average regular customers? (We call this the "conversion ratio.") This will undoubtedly vary depending on how that new customer was generated. For example, someone buying for

the first time using an aggressively priced coupon would less likely be a repeat customer than one who bought based on a personal recommendation of a friend. To be more accurate, you may want to calculate this information based on several different criteria. Then, once you have the numbers for three or four scenarios, take an average.

4. What is the average life cycle of a new customer? That is, once you get a customer, how long will that customer continue to buy from you before he or she moves, gets mad, or no longer has a need for your product or service? This length of time can generally be expressed in months or years. It may be a more difficult number to get, but do your best.

5. How many new customers are referred to you by your existing customers? When you gather information about a new customer, ask how they found out about you. One possible answer is "referred by a friend."

When calculating your return, consider that there are three main types of ROI:

1. *Immediate ROI.* This is the return you get on a given marketing event. That would be the dollars generated directly from the sales related to that promotion. In the example above, the Immediate ROI was $1,500, or 30%. It's always good when your marketing shows an immediate profit. It doesn't always work that way—$5,000 could have been spent that generated $3,000 of total sales. That's $1,500 of actual margin and a loss of $4,500.

2. *Long-term ROI.* This takes a look into all of the sales generated from a new customer over that customer's life cycle. First you need to figure out the value of a regular customer, and we'll go over that shortly.

3. *Multi-input ROI.* If your ad appears in a monthly magazine each month for a year, do your sales from each ad increase each month? If so, you may have to factor in the benefit of the repetition of that ad. Perhaps the first few insertions lost money, but by the third month, it had started generating net profits. The third ad shows a positive ROI. In such a case, you may want to calculate your ROI based on the entire schedule of ads in that publication. It's likely that the results you're getting in months 3 through 12 would not have been as strong without the first two ads that lost money.

## How to Determine the Value of a New Regular Customer

In order to figure out how much in gross sales a new regular customer brings you in a year, you need to define what a regular customer is. Through a careful audit you can determine this information. Obviously, "regulars" can range from several times a week or several times a year. So, set those criteria. For example, a typical fast, casual operation may set that number at three or four times a month, while a more upscale operation may set it at three or four times a year.

Then you simply multiply that average regular frequency number by your average check. We use the average check, not the average guest, because for local store marketing (LSM) it will be a more accurate number, in that you have one person who influences the dining decision. For the purposes of illustration, let's say that we have determined that your average regular frequency is once a week with an average check of $10. By simply multiplying 52 weeks by $10 we then have calculated that the value of a new regular customer is $520 annually. As simple as it sounds, many operators don't bother to figure this out, which means they're flying blind.

### What's Your Targeted Increase?

Simple question, but let's break it down. Let's say our sample unit does $1,000,000 in annual sales. The goal for the year is to show an increase of 5% in gross sales. $50,000 in additional sales attributable to LSM is needed.

### How Many New Regulars Do You Need to Hit Your Sales Target?

Now we divide the sales goal of $50,000 by the value of a new regular customer ($520). And the answer is 96.1. You need 96.1 new regular customers to generate $50,000 in additional sales.

### What's Your Conversion Ratio?

There's just one more important piece of the LSM puzzle now. How many first-time buyers does it take to generate one new regular customer? In our experience it will range from as low as 12% to around 25%, though it can be as high as 50% for newer locations with super operations. The point here is you should not guess. The research tells you with certainty what you have to work with so you have no illusions of what it's going to take to make your sales numbers. Let's say you determine that you get a 25% conversion ratio. You know you need 193 new regulars to hit your goals. Therefore you need four times as many "first-time buyers" to end up with 193 regulars. Simply put, by bringing in *772 first-time buyers* (under the right circumstances) you are very likely to end up with 193 new regular customers. Those 193 will generate an additional $50,000 in this year and another $50,000 in the following year. So your goal will be attract between 64 and 65 first-timers each month on average.

Use the simple worksheet in Figure 3.1 to help calculate exactly how many first-time buyers you need to capture enough new regular customers to reach a specific sales target increase.

**FIGURE 3.1:** Sales Target Increase Worksheet

|  | **Example** | **Your Unit** |
|---|---|---|
| 1. What are your annual sales? | $1,000,000 | |
| 2. What is your percent targeted increase? | 5% | |
| Gross sales increase needed in dollars | $50,000 | |
| 3. What is your average sale per transaction? | $10.00 | |
| 4. What is your annual customer value? | $520.00 | |
| What is your conversion ratio? | 25% | |
| How many first-time buyers needed to reach goal? | 772 | |

Simply plug in the answers to questions 1 through 4 with proper formula for the other cells.

## What About Those "Old" Regular Customers?

There is one other piece that is often more difficult to get a handle on. How many of those regular customers who received your promotional piece increased their frequency as a result of the promotion? If a given promotion generated 100 redemptions and 25 of those were first-time buyers, how do you evaluate the effect of the remaining 75? One view is that they would have come in anyway and paid full price. In that case those 75 redemptions cost you money. Or, did they come in one more time than they would have otherwise as a result of the promotion? In that case they made you money. Without some good consumer research it's really hard to tell. But ideally, knowing that piece of information helps you fine-tune your ROI numbers.

For example, let's say you ran a $2 savings promotion. Fifty of your 100 redemptions were regular customers who would have come in anyway. That cost you $100 right off the bottom line. No benefit. The remaining 25 regulars came in one more

## NO B.S. GRASSROOTS MARKETING INCONVENIENT TRUTH #5

"Money Math" is NOT simple or easy. But getting it right
is essential to winning as a David against Goliaths,
to getting more productivity from
every invested dollar.

time than usual. They spent $8 more than usual as a result of that promotion. That's $200 more in gross sales. So the net gain of the 75 regulars was $100 in additional gross sales. Granted, the margin will be less, but if those were the actual numbers, the extra $100 doesn't hurt. But it's those 25 first-time buyers that we're actually looking for.

At a 25% conversion ratio, you should end up with 6.25 new regular customers from that single promotion. Since we know that a regular customer is worth $520 on average annually, you will eventually generate $3,350 in increased gross sales from the promotion (taking into account the discount on the regulars).

If that promotion was an average one for you, then you should be trending up at 5% after about 14 to 15 promotions.

The next phase is then to determine the response rate you get from the various LSM tactics you'll use to hit your goal. Once you begin to know those numbers, you have a clear picture of just how many of what type of promotions you need to do over the course of your year to hit your goal. At the same time, you probably want to look at ways to improve your conversion ratio. That will allow you to get more results from each promotion you set up as well as your traditional advertising, plus better retention and frequency from your existing customers.

### The Complexities of Multi-Input ROI

Making these calculations is more complicated when you mix the media. It is possible for a customer to see your front sign, read a newspaper ad, observe several of your delivery trucks with your logo, talk to a friend who recommends you, and then look you up in the Yellow Pages. When that customer is asked, "How did you find out about us?" he might respond with the last marketing contact, "Yellow Pages." But that sale would not have happened if it weren't for most, if not all, of those previous impressions.

The point is that capturing this information is not perfect. Just be aware of the limitations as you begin to put the information to use.

## How to Use Tracking Devices with Your Grassroots Marketing Pieces

Tracking the results of each of your promotions is critical in determining how well your marketing is working. The proper tracking devices help you more easily incorporate tracking as part of your regular operation.

### Redemption

Redemption of a printed piece that has value when used in a purchase is an easy and accurate way of evaluating printed forms of marketing, including print media, direct mail, group coupon mailers, etc.

Consider Steve, the manager of a Back Yard Burger in Tennessee. He arranged for a Blockbuster down the street to hand out a coupon to each of their customers for one week. To get the special price, a customer had to come in with the cross-promotion certificate. The number of certificates redeemed tells you only half the story. There were about 200 redemptions. But not all that came in were new customers.

Steve simply had his counter people ask everyone who redeemed the Blockbuster certificate if it was their first visit; if they said they were first-time diners, the counter person marked it on the certificate. They also attached that certificate to the receipt of the sale. In that way Steve could determine exactly, to the penny, the level of new immediate sales that were generated from that promotion. His bounce-back coupon also allowed him to determine who came in for a second time.

Figure 3.2 shows a cross-promotion that generated nearly 100 first-time buyers for this restaurant using a minimal investment and both time and money.

To analyze the true value of a promotion, distill the number of new customers from the redemptions. If you have a regular customer already, you don't want to discount that regular customer if he or she would have been willing to pay full price to begin with. This point is more important for marketing on a local level. Another consideration is whether the frequency of visits of a regular customer was increased by that customer's use of the certificate.

You've probably figured that his ROI was very high, since the cost of the entire promotion was about $25. These types of lower-cost alternatives to more expensive media advertising will be explored in later chapters.

When you get down to it, there are really only four ways to increase your sales on a local level:

1. Increase your customer count (get more customers).
2. Increase your customer frequency (get them to buy more often).

**FIGURE 3.2:** Restaurant Cross-Promotion

3. Increase your average transaction value (get them to spend more money each time).
4. Convert current purchases into more products or services with higher profit margins.

If your marketing tactic positively impacts one or all of these four areas, you can show a strong return, which we refer to as "worthy ROI."

Any degree of worthy ROI will usually involve tracking your marketing tactic in one of four ways:

1. The number of visits to your location.
2. The number of inbound phone calls.

3. The number of mail-in, fax, or email requests or orders.

4. The number of unique visitors that log on to your website.

All four of these require a "call to action" in the marketing proposition. In turn, each action allows you to gather the information you need to begin to determine the quantitative value of your marketing. With e-commerce, for example, you can easily track where all your sales came from, as well as the activity the customer does on your site.

Direct mail and direct response advertising, where the product is purchased directly as a result of the advertisement, is also easily tracked. The challenge comes from most other forms of marketing that are not as easily tracked. Here are some common approaches that can help you begin to get an idea of what level of sales is generated from which marketing approaches.

- *Redemption.* A coupon is the one of the easiest ways of tracking. It has to accompany the purchase. It generally saves money or increases value, giving the customer a reason to bring it in. Determining if the coupon user is a new customer or not requires more effort, though. You must train your frontline staff to ask the question, "Is this your first time in our store?" The answer then needs to be recorded on the coupon or on a tally sheet. Whether a customer is new or existing is an important piece of information for getting a real, accurate ROI. Discounting your regular customers, who probably would have paid full price anyway, is not the best way to increase your sales. It's okay to do that when necessary, however. If a given coupon promotion has 100 redemptions and generates 10 new customers, it's probably going to have a positive ROI.
- *Advertising codes and extension numbers.* For print advertising, including newspaper, magazine, and direct mail, you can use a promotional code, unique phone number, or

email address to determine which ad was responsible for customer contact. In your call to action, include the special code. If the reader is taking advantage of a special offer in your ad, they must give you the promotional code to receive the offer. The code tells you which ad generated the sale.

For a coupon or ad that is either mailed in or brought to your location, the code is still important. You can run the same ad in several publications over a period of time. By making the promotional code unique to each insertion, you can track which publication or edition brought in the business.

Once you know the medium responsible for the contact, you can track the purchases of that contact to figure out the ROI for that ad. Getting several hundred phone calls is not enough. How many of those phone calls resulted in sales? Only when you know that can you figure out if the ads are really working for you.

- *Specific to product.* When introducing a new product or service, gross sales of that product or service can easily be compared to the cost of generating those sales. Steve at Backyard Burger started a kids' night on Wednesdays. Kids eat free when accompanied by a paying adult. He brought in a clown, toy giveaways, and a Moonwalk inflatable each Wednesday, spending an additional $150 for the extras. (He was able to get a trial rate for the inflatable Moonwalk for four weeks of $50 per week including setup). The marketing was done internally to existing customers and on an outside marquee sign. Assuming he's running a 50% profit on food, paper, and labor costs, he needs to generate at least $300 more on a Wednesday to break even. With an increase of, let's say, $600, there would be a ROI of 25% on gross sales ($150 cost into $600 in additional sales). That's pretty strong. So, in this case, the increase in sales came mainly from existing customers buying more often.

It's possible with this type of tracking method that you'll get more response than you will actually record. A customer might have intended to bring his children one night but couldn't for some reason. Yet because he had top-of-mind awareness as a result of the promotion, he may come in the next day for lunch. In that case, the kids' program would have generated an additional sale at lunchtime but it would not likely be included in any tracking program except the macro-ROI calculations.

- *Specific call to action.* In your advertising, ask the consumers to take a specific course of action. It could be to call a certain number or visit a website. You could get a rough idea by comparing the overall volume of calls or hits prior to the marketing program with those after the marketing program. Or you could provide the consumers with a specific number to call or URL to visit, which would give you a more accurate take on the activity generated from the marketing.

- *Unique toll-free numbers.* Toll-free numbers are very inexpensive. They are simply forwarded into your regular phone lines. Most vendors only charge you for the actual calling time used on the inbound call. The advantage is that if you assign a certain toll-free number to a specific marketing campaign, any calls on that number are automatically tracked for you. Your monthly bill will even give a list of phone numbers that were used in calling your toll-free number. This setup is not only good for tracking, but also for creating a very inexpensive follow-up marketing program, including enhancing your database marketing program.

- Consumer research can determine if there is an increase in overall awareness of a product, service, or business. The problem is that it is very costly and generally can't be applied to specific advertising. So for most small businesses, it is impractical to use. However, as a savvy No-B.S. Marketer you might get a local college that offers a marketing research course to take you on as a class project. Just make sure that the questionnaire they use will not bias the answers you get.

## Managing Your Tracking Initiative

In your business, you need to have your frontline people ask the questions and document the results. It has to be clear that this is not a volunteer assignment. Make it easy for them with a simple tracking sheet that requires very few entries. I prefer to use one that uses simple tick marks so it takes a minimal amount of time for the counter people or inbound phone staff to capture that information.

## NO B.S. GRASSROOTS MARKETING INCONVENIENT TRUTH #6

If you can't track it, it don't hack it. Without tracking the results of your marketing, you will never know how to get the absolute most from your marketing dollars.

You also will need to spot-check their efforts. Just because you tell them they must record this information doesn't mean it will get done. I suggest a carrot-and-stick method. Send a "mystery shopper" into your place. If the counter person does the marketing data capture properly, the mystery shopper hands over a $20 bill on the spot; word will get out that staff should be on their toes. Conversely, if the counter person does not capture the data properly, the shopper hands over a memo in the shape of a $20 bill that tells that person he or she just lost out a nice spiff. Likewise, the word will get out real quick.

For the phone staff, it should work similarly. The manager could have an envelope with a $20 bill in it. Only the mystery phone shopper and the manager would know the secret password. When the phone staff captures the right information, the caller identifies himself/herself and tells the phone staff the password so he/she can tell the supervisor. The envelope is handed over on the spot. But if the phone staff does not handle the call properly, the phone staff is given a different password. The supervisor hands over a different envelope over with a note explaining that it could have been a $20 bill.

## Managing the Untrackable

What if you have a marketing program that has no effective way of being tracked?

First, you need to assess the level of risk involved. For a local business, if such a program costs $10,000, that would be high risk. If it costs $50, it's low risk. Obviously, you have to adjust the number for your marketplace and business. For the higher risk marketing ventures that are not traceable, the answer is simple. Stop it. If you can't track it, don't do it. On the other hand, if it costs you very little money and time, and you have a good feeling about it, my advice is the same: Stop it.

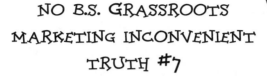

# *NO B.S. GRASSROOTS MARKETING INCONVENIENT TRUTH #7*

There are lots and lots and lots of things you can do with advertising, marketing, and promotion, but just because you can, doesn't mean you should. Do what you do for the right reason. Be wary of investing in things because they are popular, are normal and customary, are what "everybody" does, "cool kids" do, or giants do. Be resistant to pressure by media salespeople, marketing "gurus" biased to or selling particular tools, and employees, peers, friends, and family. Not everyone has your best interests in mind. Not everyone with opinions has qualified opinions. It is YOUR responsibility to hold each investment and activity up to harsh assessment and measurement, to minimize risks, avoid waste, and obtain positive returns.

With limited budgets you can't afford to guess what works and what doesn't. Only choose those marketing approaches that have the ability to prove their value to you. If it's not provable, it's not valuable.

There may be marketing that is not provable that works great. The problem is you'll never know it. For local businesses, you have to be picky about where you put your limited resources for marketing.

Once you've figured out all these numbers related to your marketing, you will have a valuable piece of information at your disposal. It's like knowing the actual cost of the car to the dealer before negotiating the final price. The calculations tell you several things. First, they let you know if you're making improvements in the efficiency of your marketing. Second, it gives you a guide when evaluating the cost of a new marketing program. If that radio salesperson comes to you with a $5,000 proposal, you may now know that it only makes sense to you if that investment can generate, let's say, $15,000 worth of sales. You know from past experience that it has generated about $10,000 in sales. Given that, you should only be willing to pay $3,330 for that schedule to make it work for you. If the rep doesn't play ball, you simply walk away and find an alternative marketing approach that fits within your guidelines. Either way, you are working to improve your ROI.

# CHAPTER 4

# If You Use Mass Ad Media,
## Make Your Ad Dollars Do More

Jeff Slutsky

I t's likely that a significant portion of your marketing budget is devoted to some type of mass advertising media. As mentioned before, the ROI from mass advertising media have been eroding. Newspapers and local affiliate TV stations have been losing audience. Many radio stations have experienced the same thing. Your once single local Yellow Pages directory has spun off more clones than a Kardashian reality show. Even so, the audience sizes are still significant enough to make a major impact in your marketplace. The problem is the cost.

If the cost to reach each 1,000 members of a target audience allows you to show a good return on your investment, then the mass media is a great way to go. But what's been happening is that rates continue to rise in the face of these declining audience numbers. In short, it costs more to buy less. It's like increasing the cost of a Snickers candy bar while at the same time decreasing the weight. It now takes a Snickers plus a Mounds bar to provide the same amount of sugar rush.

Another problem is that the overall level of advertising pollution is increasing, which means that the audiences have become immune and intolerant to the advertising. They are less likely to respond to an ad now than they were years ago. Therefore, it takes more advertising weight to accomplish the same goals. That is, you would have to run many more commercials to the same audience to ensure that it's getting your message.

Despite these challenges, mass media, and in particular broadcast (network-affiliated) TV, is still the most efficient way to deliver an advertising message to a broad-based audience. The No-B.S. Marketer Solution to this dilemma is to discover how to buy your local mass advertising media so that it becomes cost effective to you. This is done in two ways. First, you learn to pay less to reach each 1,000 audience members. Second, once you reach them you must deliver a message that will get noticed, remembered, and acted upon.

The possible silver lining in the segmentation of the media is that in some cases it may be easier for a smaller or niche business to zero in on a target audience. Mass media is best at reaching a large percentage of the population. But for most local businesses, a very small subset of that population is a primary target for reaching potential customers.

## A Radical Possibility: The Big Cut

Arbitrarily cut your media budget in half. Now your task is to get the same results with the remaining half of your budget. With this move, you will not accept having half of the media exposure. You have to be a No-B.S. Marketer. You will use your wits, your knowledge, and your guts to make the remaining half of your ad budget do the same job as before the cut. So what do you do with the half you cut? Take 10% of it and use it on other proven No-B.S. Marketer tactics to supplement your advertising. And with what is left over, go on a vacation, buy a new car, pay off your loans, or even buy a couple dozen copies of this book and hand them out to your business friends. It's your money. You worked hard for it. Don't waste it on advertising that doesn't work.

## How to Make TV Deliver More

One simple way to make a big impact with a small budget is to "link" your commercial to the content of a given show. Normally you need to run a commercial repeatedly to make any headway. But if your product or service is the topic of a particular TV show, it only takes a few commercials to get your same results, because the show sells the benefits of the offering. Your commercial simply informs them where to buy it in your marketplace.

Imagine that you discovered in advance that your local morning TV station is doing an upcoming show on makeovers. Your hair salon, dress boutique, nail salon, makeup counter, weight loss clinic, or plastic surgery or cosmetic dentistry practice could promote the same type of service. It may only take a 10-second spot, or billboard, to do so. You may have to pay a premium for getting those several "fixed positions" specifically in the commercial breaks of that show, but that viewing audience would be more predisposed to buying those services.

The same could be said for marketing cruise lines during reruns of *The Love Boat* or an old romantic movie that takes place on a cruise. It would not probably work with airings of *Titanic*,

*The Poseidon Adventure* (both versions), or the made-for-TV movie about the *Achille Lauro*. *Gilligan's Island* might be a toss-up.

## How to Make All Ad Dollars Do More

Certain types of media allow you to present your message in more persuasive ways. A boat dealer can use an odd-sized newspaper ad of 6 columns wide by only 2 or 3 inches tall. That short but wide sized ad is a great dimension for showing off a photo of a boat. Some radio stations and some cable channels can coordinate the running of your spots to specific circumstances. For example, a heating and air conditioning dealer wants their radio commercials to run only when the humidity reaches 50% or greater or when the temperature exceeds 85 degrees. Those commercials play when the listeners are likely to be in the most discomfort and therefore predisposed to considering getting help. A car wash runs their commercials only when the prediction is for sunshine for the next two days or greater. Pizza delivery runs more commercials on rainy days when they know their business is likely to pick up. A tire dealer pushes snow tires when there's two or more inches of snow predicted. Auto body repair runs their spots when there's ice or hail warnings and other hazardous driving conditions. My karate instructor used to run his advertising on TV when the FBI would come out with their latest statistics on violent crime. His message was marketing self-defense and personal safety.

Before buying any kind of mass media you must first really understand who your customers are. The more you can identify your customers demographically, psychographically, and geographically, the easier it is to buy media that is most likely to reach them. This saves you a tremendous amount of money in the long run while making your advertising a lot more effective.

In addition to going through your database and identifying your clients by zip codes, you can also conduct inexpensive surveys. Have an employee call your customers or stand in front of your building with a clipboard and ask them questions as they leave. Find out their pasttimes, hobbies, favorite radio station, favorite TV show, what kind of car they drive, etc. One quick oil change place listed all the major radio stations at the bottom of their worksheet/invoice. While in the car checking the odometer, they also circled the radio station that the radio was tuned to. If they had time, they would even mark off the radio stations that preset buttons were programmed to. This gave them an indication as to what stations their customers listened to.

Gain additional insights about your customers by having your media reps provide you with a Scarborough report for your industry, in your market. Scarborough Research measures the shopping patterns, lifestyles, and media habits of consumers locally, regionally, and nationally; Scarborough measurements detail the lives of American adults. According to their website, www.scarborough.com, Scarborough Research's core services include 75 local market studies and a national database. These tools cover 1,700 categories and brands including comprehensive retail shopping behaviors, lifestyle characteristics, in-depth consumer demographics, and media usage patterns.

## *Critical Mass*

Reaching "critical mass," as a marketing concept, means you are sure you have bought enough media exposure in a specific period to do the job. Any less than what you need to spend is a waste of money. If you can't afford enough media to make a difference, then simply save your money and wait until you can afford to get enough. For a daily newspaper, never buy less than a quarter-page ad. Anything smaller gets lost. For that reason it's suggested that you don't buy the "awareness builder" program where you get two columns by two inches a couple of times a week for a year or two. In broadcast media, critical mass is around 150 gross rating points (GRP) per week. If you can only afford 75 GRPs, concentrate your ads into three days. If you can't afford that, bank the money.

When applying critical mass to cable, be sure you get the gross rating points based on the DMA not the CDMA. The CDMA is the cable industry's version of the Neilson "Designated Market Area." Only, unlike a true DMA, the CDMA only counts those households that have cable. This makes their numbers look better than they really area. If you want to compare a cable buy to a broadcast TV buy, make sure your cable advertising rep uses the DMA numbers.

## *Know Your SQAD*

Established in the 1970s, the former Spot Quotations and Data, Inc., legally changed its name to the acronym SQAD in 2001. To know if you're getting a fair price for your advertising, compare your CPP (cost per point) for your targeted demographic group against the SQAD rating at www.sqad.com. SQAD collects real costs for national and local radio and TV stations. A good independent media buyer will subscribe to this service. Consider using one to help you negotiate all these variables and place the media for you. As I like to say, "If you don't know SQAD, then you don't know squat!" These numbers will tell you what businesses and agencies are actually paying for specific day parts and specific stations and shows.

## *Custom TV Tags*

The major cable companies are starting to incorporate technology that allows a commercial to be played with a different tag in each zone. Eventually you should be able to buy a zone spot on cable. The advantage of this is a number of different dealers or franchisees can buy cable and focus geographically in a specific area. Currently you can expect to pay a 30% premium for this service, but if you pull your business from that zone only, it is actually cheaper to reach your target audience. If you pull from two or more zones, you're better off buying the entire coverage area.

## Stick It

Daily newspapers can zone as well. One way to generate immediate awareness of your sales event, for example, is with a sticky note on the front page of the paper. There's usually no other advertising on the front page. The sticky note provides maximum readership of a very short, simple message. Plus it can be zoned usually down to the zip code. It may appear expensive; however, given the ability to target geographically with a high-impact, high-readership device, your ROI could be very attractive. A downside of this tool is that it requires a longer lead time.

## Other People's Ad Money

In an effort to rein in the cost of your advertising, one of the best solutions is to get someone else to pay for all or part of your advertising. Co-op advertising provides a lot of opportunity for retailers to get help underwriting their advertising. The amount of co-op advertising available to you from your vendors usually depends on a percentage of the product you buy. The same rules have to apply to all the merchants as a result of the Robinson Packman Act. But there are ways to get a bigger allotment of co-op funds.

Most manufacturers or distributors have a special fund set aside called MDF, or market development funds. You can approach the zone manager of a vendor with a professionally thought-out proposal of how you wish to sell a certain amount of units using a certain advertising campaign. Let's say you plan to get $50,000 of advertising to achieve this goal. You want a particular vendor to put up perhaps $25,000 of it, even though you've already used up all your co-op funds. By convincing the regional honcho of the benefits of your plan, you stand a good chance of getting that support. Plus, if you can negotiate a special deal with the media that allows you to buy the proposed exposure for less, a greater portion of your outlay will be reimbursed, as a percentage.

A variation of the co-op advertising program is done by a local award program, The Consumers' Choice Award. A select group of the best businesses in their category agree to buy a license to use the award in their advertising and marketing. As a licensee, they each qualify to participate in a TV advertising campaign that announces their win to the area consumers. This is done with a 30-second doughnut spot, where the middle 15 seconds is specifically about the licensee's company. The cost of participating is about 30% percent less per rating point than the SQAD rating. That means that they are getting local TV airtime on several network affiliates, one independent, and some cable channels at a greatly reduced rate. Additionally, there are dozens of other businesses also running their spots. Awareness of the award campaign increases dramatically as does that of the individual winners. In this situation, a number of seemingly unrelated businesses band together through a special program. With this collection of businesses, our media buyer, Brad, had tremendous leverage with the local media to negotiate the rates. Of course participation in this type of program is limited to only those businesses that win the award. The same program has also been done with quarter-page ads in a newspaper insert. The key point is that when TV or newspaper becomes cost prohibitive there might be ways to join forces with other noncompetitive businesses to pool enough money to motivate the media to be more flexible.

## Buy Smarter to Sell More for Less

The last piece of the local advertising media puzzle is your ability to buy it for less. Assuming you really know your target audience and you have a message that will cause them to act, your job now is to get as much exposure to the right people as possible, given your limited budget. For local advertising, Marshal McLuhan had it all wrong when he said the medium is the message. The No B.S. Grassroots Marketing Solution states that the "medium is the driver of the message." You don't have to have a super entertaining or funny ad to get results. But you do have to have an ad that appeals to the potential buyer with enough benefits to create interest. The more exposure you get for your message given the same budget, the greater potential for a return on your marketing investment.

When you buy radio advertising, after you've negotiated the best deal you think you can get, ask for matching commercials that can run any time during the 24 hours they're on the air. Even a spot at 3:00 A.M. will have some listeners. If that spot is free, it can only help you with your ROI. The worst they can tell you is "No." I used to ask for matching overnight spots, to which the stations would often agree. This is the time from midnight to 5:59 A.M. Once they agreed to it, I ask them to "bracket" those spots between 5:00 and 5:59 A.M. They usually could put a portion of them during that time frame. At 6:00 A.M. begins the morning drive, when you'll pay a premium. But at 5:59 you're still in overnight and paying nothing. The audience size doesn't increase a hundredfold in the five or ten minutes before 6:00 A.M. You will pick up a little bit of extra audience that way.

I always tell my clients, when you have a limited ad budget, don't buy the number-one station in town. Because they're so successful they will likely be less willing to provide you a better deal than perhaps the third- or fourth-ranked stations. In most markets, the top-ranked radio station, at the most, has 20% of the radio listening market. That means you can buy 80% of the market by using everyone else if you wanted to. The determining factor for which stations you should put your money on is your CPM (cost per thousand). This is the cost to reach each 1,000 listeners in your target audience.

By way of illustration, let's compare the cost of reaching 1,000 listeners to gallons of gasoline. You know if gasoline sells for $3.00 per gallon at one station and $3.10 at another, where you get more bangs for your buck. The second gas station may have three times as much gas in their inventory as the first station. Who cares? You're only concerned about what it cost you for the 15 or so gallons you need for your car. CPM is to radio as cost per gallon is to gasoline. Now, a third gas station may offer gas at $2.75 per gallon but they only have five gallons in inventory. That doesn't solve your problem. You could buy the five but then go back to the first station to fill up your tank. Or you may decide it's not worth the effort, but you know in any case exactly what you're getting for your money.

This may be a little too simplistic a metaphor. However, make sure you are selecting the radio stations based on the best price to reach your target audience, not on what station you listen to, or if the station is giving away a free trip if you buy a certain amount of air time, or the rep is cute. If you're buying for any other reason than a good CPM, you're probably paying too much.

Let's say your target audience is *women between the ages of 25 and 54*. I had this same target audience when I dated before I got married. The number one rated radio station in town may not be number one for that particular demographic. So only look at the numbers for your target audience. Any audience that you pay for outside of your target is a waste of your money.

### Frequency

When buying radio time, you want the audience to hear your spot at least five times. It takes five or more hits before a person will absorb

---

enough of your message to act on it. If a station wants you to pay a certain cost per spot so that you can't get enough total commercials (frequency), then you need to rethink the buy. Either concentrate on cheaper day parts or a less expensive station. Purchasing one or two spots during drive time is a waste of money, regardless of the audience size. There's not enough critical mass to do the job.

Figure 4.1 is a comparison of four different fictional radio stations. Station One has the most total audience in the target, but they are also charging the most to reach each listener. With a budget of $1,000 you could buy 13 commercials. That may not be enough repetition to do the job for you. On Station Two, you can buy 50 commercials. The audience is half the size, but you can dominate that group. Using a combination of Stations Two, Three, and Four, you can still reach 35,000 in your target with enough frequency to do the job. Therefore, the largest audience isn't always the best audience for you.

There are additional factors to consider. The station's format plays into the mix as well as one other number, called "CUME." CUME is the total number of different people who have tuned into that day part. The audience level, or *average quarter hour*, is how many people are tuned into that station at a point in time.

**FIGURE 4.1:** Largest Audience May Not be Best Audience for You

| Station | Women 25–54 | Cost per Spot | Cost per Thousand |
|---|---|---|---|
| Station One | 50,000 | $75.00 | $1.50/M |
| Station Two | 25,000 | $20.00 | $.80/M |
| Station Three | 10,000 | $11.00 | $1.10/M |
| Station Four | 5,000 | $5.00 | $1.00/M |

Since you know you need a person to hear your commercial at least five times, a station with a more loyal audience is more likely to hear your spot repeatedly than a station with a fickle audience. Look for the relationship between quarter hour and CUME. The lower the ratio the less turnover that station has. Less turnover means you can use fewer commercials to achieve the same results as a station with a higher turnover.

The weekly newspaper can be an affordable alternative to your daily newspaper. Just because you don't read it doesn't mean your potential customers don't. There are thousands of successful weekly newspapers, so they must be doing something right. It certainly deserves a test. Suburban papers do a great job of reporting on neighborhood news. They are distributed in zones so you can reach a more geographically suitable area. For a fair test, use no less than a half-page ad. Test one zone only at first. And use a strong call to action, preferably with a coupon or a special offer if they call, so you can track the results.

If you find that the suburban papers work for you, and you work with them on a regular basis, you might also have some leverage to suggest an article about your company to get some additional free exposure.

The local business journal is a weekly paper that reaches members of the business community. Before using them, however, pay close attention to your cost per thousand compared to the business section of your local daily newspaper. I was considering using a business journal in one Midwestern market. Their circulation was around 15,000 and they claimed a pass-along readership of about 3.5. The local daily newspaper had a weekday subscription of around 200,000. The business section generally gets about 65% of the readership, which would make it around 130,000. The cost of a quarter-page ad in the daily was twice that of the weekly business journal. But the cost per thousand was so much lower. Even though the journal zeroed in the target audience we were looking for, the daily also reached much of that same audience plus a lot more. Of course the only way to know for sure is to test and track both.

## Negotiate

Most media will negotiate a better price under the right circumstances. The cost is directly related to supply and demand. If the station has a lot of unsold air time or a publication has a lot of unsold space, you're more likely to convince them to give you a special price. For TV, stay away during election times. Politicians eat up a lot of airtime and the stations are required by the FCC to sell it to them at the lowest rate they offer any other advertiser. Ratings sweeps are also bad times to get deals, as is fall, when the new lineup of mediocre network shows comes out. The bigger your budget, the more the station is generally willing to work with you on pricing.

For radio or TV, use the SQAD ratings of the shows or day parts as your guide to know what kind of deal you should ask for. If the average SQAD rate is $50 per rating point, you want to ask for half that. But if you get at least a 25% discount off of the SQAD rate, you're doing well. So in this example, anything from $25 to $37 per rating point would be acceptable. If a station is not willing to meet your conditions, go to another station. You can achieve your advertising objectives through a variety of approaches, so look at all the alternatives and associated prices to determine the most cost-effective way to go. If the local TV stations won't play ball, check your daily newspaper, radio stations, and cable. Perhaps a combination of several of those media can do the job better, given your budget.

## A Dirty Little Trick

This radio negotiation tactic was actually taught to me by a radio salesman. For some reason, when I share this in seminars, there is always one audience member who is offended. I personally feel it's your duty to get the most you can from any mass media, so at the risk of being shunned, give this a try if you want more for your radio dollars.

First of all, this works best on smaller stations in smaller markets. When the rep first visits your business, give him/her a flat amount of money to work with. If you want to spend, let's say, $2,500, then you stick with it. The rep is paid a commission based on the gross sale. So if you try to get the schedule for $2,000, they think they just lost money. Instead, you want to negotiate more spots, better times, bonus spots, and other extras. But leave the budget alone.

When I'm talking with the rep, I want them to quote the schedule based on 30-second spots. They're usually about 20% less than 60 seconds so I get a little more frequency. I always provide the station the spot so I can control. When the rep comes to pick up the spot I provide a 60-second spot in a 30-second box. The rep calls back in a panic about an hour later and tells me I made a big mistake. I always apologize and tell them how bad I feel about screwing up. I always buy 60s! Which is true. I always buy 60s (but negotiate for 30s). I tell them I don't have any more budget and I already got the 60s approved by my partner (or boss, or head office, etc.). "Is there any way we let this slide this one time?" At that point the rep does not want to lose the commission. So he/she goes back to the station and starts selling his/her boss on why we should let it slide. Believe it or not, it almost always works—once.

Now that I've doubled my airtime, I stand a much better chance of getting some results from my schedule. And if it works, I become a regular customer. Win-win. And if it tanks, I write that rep a glowing testimonial. Why? I want him to sell as much of that worthless airtime to my competitors as possible.

## *Remnants of an Effective Medium*

One way to get a station to want to work with you is if you can provide total flexibility in placing your schedule. A two-to-three-week window works pretty well for this. You leave it up to the station to run it in the major day parts (prime, fringe, news, late night, daytime, early morning) in the days they have availabilities. You can even offer to buy up any unsold airtime over a period of time, in certain day parts, at a specific price per spot. This may sound like, "I'll buy all unsold spots in the month of May, between 3 P.M. and 11:30 P.M., at $50 per spot up to 100 commercials." Be sure to put a cap on it. This is called buying remnants. The same strategy can also work in print.

If you are already using a certain station or publication, they usually will not be willing to allow you to buy in this manner, since you've already set a precedent with your ad buying. This strategy would work better if you want to make a major shift in your advertising. If you usually buy a lot of newspaper ads, the TV stations may be willing to play ball with you because they'll see it as found business.

## *Seasonality*

If you have a seasonal business it is futile to attempt, through advertising, to get people to buy in the off season. Nobody is going to buy a boat in Michigan in January. The best you can hope to do is extend your season a few weeks on either side of the cycle and perhaps prop it up a little bit at the peak. Advertising when people are not in the market to buy is a waste of money. Extending the sales cycle a little is called "broadening the shoulders," and refers to the bell curve of the sales cycle, as shown in Figure 4.2 on page 62.

No matter what approach you take to your advertising, as stated many times before, it is critical to track your results. Even

FIGURE **4.2:** "Broadening the Shoulders" to Extend Your Sales
Cycle Before and After the Optimum Selling Season

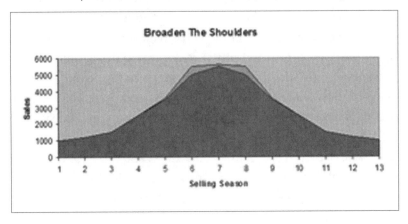

if you have a campaign that totally bombs, you've learned what not to do in the future. There is always a certain amount of trial and error in advertising. Stick with what works and dump what doesn't.

## Yellow Pages Directories

As I mentioned earlier, I hear more complaints and horror stories from businesspeople about the Yellow Pages than any other form of advertising. Yellow Pages advertising is one of the only advertising media where you're listed with all your competitors. When customers let their fingers do the walking, it means you'll get a lot of phone callers, but most of them are price shopping. Unless you know how to handle an inbound inquiry generated from Yellow Pages advertising, you may not get a chance to sell to a given customer.

That fact, that all your competitors are listed with you, leads to one of my biggest pet peeves. Don't put "Look for our ad in the Yellow Pages" on any other form of advertising. When other forms or advertising are doing their job, why would you direct those potential buyers to a place that also features your competition?

More recently, there has been a proliferation of Yellow Pages. If you need to use this type of advertising, you're probably best served by going in the main utility directory. Stay out of "the other book" and also avoid those neighborhood books.

Now, more than ever, it's critical to track your Yellow Pages advertising results. The younger generation, which is very computer savvy, is more likely to search for a supplier, vendor, or service provider via the internet than to schlep out that heavy directory. As the younger computer-focused generation ages, this trend may continue to erode the value of your Yellow Pages advertising.

Ad size is another factor. Yellow Pages reps have a reputation for really pushing for bigger ads. If all your major competition has a large ad, you may need one, too. But you don't have to be the biggest ad there. You just want a good representation so that potential buyers know you exist. The trick is to design your ad so that it catches their eye. Size alone is not necessary for that.

Treat your Yellow Pages ad like any other ad. Don't let the rep design it for you. Hire a professional. You are going to have to live with that ad for an entire year, whether or not it works for you. Don't take the chance. Use a strong benefit headline. Make it clear in your ad why you have an advantage over your competition. Also have a strong call to action. Color adds to the expense, so try seeing if the ad pulls just as many good leads without color.

You may find that if you reduce the size of your ad, the Yellow Pages people will punish you by moving you deeper in your section. So if you're just starting out, it's best to start small. Test. Then, based on the verified results, you can increase the size and test again.

One of my favorite Yellow Pages stories happened many years ago. In Colorado there was a small independent pizza chain owned by a family. They specialized in delivery. They lived and died by Yellow Pages advertising because back then if you wanted a pizza delivered, you looked in the Yellow Pages under "pizza." They had a small ad that appeared on page three of the pizza section, and it worked fine. Then, a few years later, Domino's Pizza started their expansion into their territory. Domino's had a much bigger ad budget and even bought a full-page ad. Naturally, Domino's ended up on page one in the pizza section. On the back of that ad were four major competitors. And the independent, family-owned operation was shoved deeper into the section, so much so that as soon as the new Yellow Pages was released, his sales dropped dramatically.

What could the owner do? He couldn't compete toe-to-toe with Domino's. But he was a No-B.S. Marketer. His solution was to run a campaign that said, "Bring us the Domino's Yellow Pages ad, out of the phone book, and I'll give you 2-for-1 pizzas!" People were ripping them out and bringing them in. After that campaign, you were hard pressed to find a Domino's Yellow Pages ad anywhere in their market. Domino's was upset. They had to pay for that ad for another 11 months.

### *Redirect the Number*

There is one other example of a creative use of a directory. I was giving a breakout session following my keynote speech for Super 8 Motels at their annual convention in New Orleans. One of the franchisees told me that a big problem they were having was that customers would confuse them with Motel 6. Many times customers would call directory assistance and ask for Motel 8, intending to call Super 8 Motels. More times than not the operator would tell them that there was no Motel 8 but there was a Motel 6. I suggested that they buy a supplemental listing under the name Motel 8. Back then the cost to add another listing was just about $20 per month. It would be listed in the phone book, but more importantly, directory assistance would have that listing as well. The phone number, of course, was the same as the local Super 8 Motel. The entire group got very excited about this very simple idea.

That reminds me of the story about a guy who created a long-distance service called "I Don't Know." When a customer was asked by their local service provider which long-distance service he or she wanted, many of the responses were, "I don't know." He got all that business.

## The Bottom Line Is the Bottom Line

When looking at the mass media portion of your marketing plan, always see if there is a better, less expensive way to achieve the results you need. All mass media can be effective if executed right, but there are many variables. In the meantime you could end up spending a small fortune before you finally come up with just the right approach that works for your business.

CHAPTER 5

# Taking It to the Streets
## Neighborhood Marketing Strategies

Jeff Slutsky

O ne of the biggest areas of improvement in the ROI for many small, medium, and even large companies will come from the development and implementation of an effective neighborhood level, *grassroots* marketing program. You usually hear the term grassroots used in political campaigns where the supporters literally take their message to the streets. Their minions go door to door to personally give their selling message about their particular candidate. In the business arena this same type of approach is generally referred to by several terms including: Local Store Marketing (LSM), neighborhood marketing, and even guerrilla marketing. The potential benefits of such a program have often been explored by many organizations but usually their results fall flat. It sounds good on paper, but in execution the program falls apart. Therefore, your next No B.S. Grassroots Marketing Solution needs an actual plan of attack for developing and implementing a fully integrated, local-level marketing program that is designed to work within your organization.

## What Is Local-Level Marketing?

A local-level marketing program is a local business outreach initiative where owners, managers, and employees who work at an individual location entice the local area consumers to be regular customers. The focus is on the neighborhood or community, that geographic primary trading area where the majority of the business's customers come from. It could be a three-to-five-mile radius, but that could be bigger or smaller depending on the type of business and marketplace. At this level, the mass media is cost prohibitive on an individual unit basis.

---

### NO B.S. GRASSROOTS MARKETING INCONVENIENT TRUTH #8

Most local-level marketing programs fail not because of lack of good ideas, but because of poor follow-through and support.
—Jeff Slutsky

Commitment is more important than creativity.
—Dan Kennedy

---

Even when combining a number of units in a marketplace, the individual, local-store marketing approach, when done properly, always shows the highest return for your marketing investment.

The tactics are many, but not all of them work for every situation. Your goal is to collect a war chest of ideas that will allow you to take advantage of the hundreds of opportunities to infiltrate your local area with low-cost and even free advertising designed to generate initial trial and repeat sales. But more important than the war chest of tactics, you need a system in place in your organization to ensure proper execution. The tactics are developed for and executed by the individual unit. However, if your company has 100 franchisees, or 500 dealers, or 75 agencies, you also need to create a local-level marketing infrastructure to support that effort. Most local-level marketing programs fail, not because of a lack of ideas, but because of a lack of follow-through and support. So in addition to many of the specific promotions, it's important to develop and execute an implementation infrastructure that allows you to consistently conduct local-level marketing programs over time.

## How Is the Grassroots Marketing Solution Different?

The main emphasis is not on marketing. The marketing part is the easiest part of the program. The focus is on training and development. When most local-level marketing programs get started, the unit manager or owner is handed a manual and told to go out to the community and bump up sales. Even with a full-day seminar, it's not enough to get unit owners or managers to implement the programs. Think of it like the military. You wouldn't hand someone a gun and a helmet, point to the battlefield and tell them to engage the enemy. Soldiers are well-trained. It's unfair to expect an operations-focused person to develop marketing and sales skills on their own. They go through boot camp, specialty training, on-the-job training, certification, and so on. A similar approach is what is needed to make this type of program work.

Even with the expense of the training program, the ROI is still high because once you've developed the program and trained your local managers, you have an asset that keeps on performing for you for many years to come. Even with an acceptable amount of turnover you'll find that your ROI is very attractive.

## Why Local-Level Marketing?

It is literally the missing link from most major marketing strategies. This strategy is well-suited for large companies whose primary method of distribution is through their local dealer, agency, or franchisee network. Consider a major company like Goodyear. One of their primary distribution channels is through the 5,000 independent Goodyear dealerships. Each store may carry some competing brands, but Goodyear is their primary tire vendor. Those dealers attend Goodyear meetings and go to Goodyear conventions. They get Goodyear co-op advertising dollars and floor displays. And, at some time in their store's history, they might even get a ride on one of the three Goodyear blimps.

Those 5,000 stores serve 5,000 different neighborhood communities. This perfectly supplements the national advertising that Goodyear does to promote its brand and the marketwide advertising they do to promote all the Goodyear stores in a given TV viewing area (i.e., DMA or ADI, which is area of dominant influence). But what can that single dealer do in his community to drive more business in? He's on a limited budget, runs his own operation, and is mostly trained in the area of automotive aftermarket. Mostly they buy local newspaper advertising which features price and items. And there's nothing more exciting than finding out you can get a deal on a set of P205/65 R15s.

Now imagine if there was a program where a significant number of those 5,000 independent dealers aggressively promoted to their neighborhoods consistently over the years. That could sell a lot more tires, and the cost of those additional sales would be a fraction of the cost of using mass media.

While the concept is very easy, the execution is very involved. It is well worth the effort because the end result is that all the national, regional, and marketwide advertising they do becomes dramatically more effective. The dealer, trained in No B.S. Grassroots Marketing, is more readily able to convert those mass media Gross Rating Points and race-car sponsorships into more and more sales.

The same tactics can be used by any size local business whether or not mass media is an option. From the Fortune 500 to the small, independent business, this approach will work. It's also beneficial to the regional players as well. It doesn't matter if your company operates at 5,000 locations, 500, 50 or 5; the same tactics apply.

With No B.S. Grassroots Marketing, all players compete on a somewhat level playing field. Of course those local businesses that have the benefit of multiple locations and national and regional advertising to promote their brand still have an advantage. However, a local independent can still go head-to-head with a national presence in its neighborhood. Several years ago, Burger King launched an ill-fated advertising campaign to take on McDonald's in the so-called "burger wars." The problem was that Burger King couldn't begin to challenge McDonald's because McDonald's simply has significantly more assets. They had twice as many locations and an advertising budget significantly larger than Burger King's. The way to beat McDonald's is not in a big national campaign. It's through the equivalent of a marketing insurgency. First they should have planned a successful branding campaign with the bulk of their national advertising dollars. Then, with a small fraction of that money and a good plan, developed and executed an effective, comprehensive local neighborhood program. To do this right at that level, it would have taken two to three years. But at the end of that time, they would have had a stealth program that would have allowed individual stores to effectively compete against all of their top rivals on an individual unit basis. Plus, once developed, it would require a very small amount of money to implement.

## Who Implements Local-Level Marketing?

To be most effective, the execution of these tactics needs to be done by the person running the local unit. That could be the manager or owner, but it is the person who runs the unit on a daily basis. It doesn't matter if it's the owner of the store, or the franchisee, or the manager that works for the major corporation, as long as execution comes from the local level. Of course this raises concerns for many operationally focused businesses. They want their manager running the store and not marketing. That's a mistake. Some organizations want to hire a special person to conduct the local-level marketing, usually for several stores. That's also a mistake.

It is critical that your local manager conduct the local-level marketing program for several reasons:

- If you have to pay someone to do it for you, it is no longer cost effective.
- Secondly, to take advantage of the hundreds of low-cost local promotional opportunities, you have to be totally immersed in the local community. An outside person, who swings in once every couple of weeks and is responsible for

# Most Common Mistakes

- *Not allowing enough time to fully develop the program.*
  The developmental phase allows you to provide the rest of
  your stores a program that is much easier to implement and
  more likely to be successful sooner. Cutting the development phase too soon short-circuits that effort.

- *Expecting franchisees to implement without training and
  support.* Many times a local-level marketing program begins
  and ends with a manual and/or a seminar. These are tools
  that help kick off such a program, but it's the follow-up process that makes it successful. Remember, you are dealing
  with elements of adult learning and behavior modification.

- *Not enough support from above.* All levels of management
  must support a successful local-level marketing program
  just as if you were introducing a new product, equipment,
  or procedure. Even the highest levels of management can
  help by letting the rank and file know how much the LSM
  program can mean to the company's overall success.

- *Not allowing the one-to-one marketing element to happen.*
  Some organizations are concerned that allowing franchisees
  or store franchisees do some marketing will interfere with
  their operations. They therefore want to bring in an army
  of local-level marketing people to do it for them. This is too
  costly and ineffective. The store franchisees are in a unique
  position to have their finger on the pulse of the community.
  This is the first step in dominating the neighborhood.

# Most Common Mistakes

*continued*

- *Trying to make it more complicated than it needs to be.* When the local-level marketing program is developed by an agency or marketing group without specific local marketing experience, they focus on the tactics, ideas, manuals, etc. They have a tendency to suggest ideas that are impractical for an overworked, stressed-out franchisee or store manager.

- *Unrealistic expectations.* Local-level marketing only works in stores that have solid operations and good customer service. An effective local marketing program will run a bad operation out of business faster. But if awareness and trial are the problems, local marketing can be very effective.

- *Expecting a short-time horizon.* Local-level marketing is not an overnight program. Traceable results are slow in coming but easily sustainable. The cost per new customer is much lower than any other form of marketing except for direct referral.

a number of neighborhoods, just can't have that kind of awareness and access to the community.

- As these types of programs start to develop awareness over time, the local manager becomes known by the members of the community. This local notoriety can be leveraged to create even more effective local-level marketing.

## The Big McStake

When big companies try to implement a local store marketing program they always seem to fall flat. The reason is that this is so different than any other program that they've tried to implement in the past. Most efforts are usually a manual that they have their advertising agency develop for them. An ad agency has no idea of how to make local-level marketing work. That's not their expertise. The manual ends up on the shelf gathering dust. The process that you will use to develop and implement a powerful local-level marketing program will parallel the way your organization introduces a new product or service to the marketplace.

## The Seven-Step Plan

Putting a local-level marketing plan into place effectively requires seven different but equally important steps. Most local-level marketing programs fall apart because companies fail to execute all seven of these steps.

### *Step One:*
### *Local-Level Marketing Audit*

Before reinventing the wheel, take a look at some of the local promotions that your people are already doing. See what is getting results and fully understand how they worked. You'll also uncover some less successful promotions; understanding these will help keep you from making the same mistakes that have already been made. Get the stories behind the promotions. Find out what the specific problem was or opportunity this promotion was geared to help with. Collect the real numbers when possible. If someone says the promotion was successful, get proof. How many new customers did it generate? How many additional sales did it generate? How have sales overall been affected by the promotion? What were the real costs in both time and money to execute it?

## *Step Two:*
### *Developmental Market and Unit Selection*

This step is only for companies with a large number of units in their system. For smaller companies, you would skip this step. Select several markets with several units in each of those markets. The size of the developmental group depends on the overall size of your company, but generally about 5% to 10% of total units, but not exceeding 50 or less than 5 units. From a cost-saving standpoint it helps to select markets where there is a concentration of good units.

In each developmental market, you'll choose between five and ten stores. You select stores that are already successful. You don't want any stores participating in this phase that are not profitable or are poorly managed. You may get pressure from upper management to use this program to save the losers. However, this is the wrong time to work on those units. That will come later.

Your immediate challenges in the development phase are using "generic" promotional ideas and getting the managers to do them. At this point, these tactics don't have a proven track record within your system, even though they were successful elsewhere. The execution of these ideas *converts* the generic tactics to promotions *proven* to work specifically for your organization. Therefore, low-volume stores are a detriment to your development. You'll spend much more of your resources to get a loser to break even than you will a successful store to increase volume by the same amount. Plus the equivalent percentage growth in a good store is a lot more profitable to the overall system.

At the same time be careful of including stores that are too successful. The managers of those stores might be less cooperative with the program since they're already showing good numbers. Your best bet is to select a group of stores that are in the top half to top third in volume, but not in the top 10%. Of course, there are exceptions, but use this as a starting point. You also want to make sure that the managers of those locations are really supportive of the program.

### Step Three:
### The Initial Training Seminar

You teach your developmental group the basic No-B.S. Marketer tactics in a half- or full-day seminar. Some of these tactics are presented in the next several chapters. The manual that you create is for reinforcement only. The seminar leader takes each participant through the process, using role playing to get these managers and owners used to executing the promotions. At the same time, the supervisory level people are also learning the program.

### Step Four:
### Supervised In-Field Execution

Immediately following the seminar, you visit each unit and coach the manager or owner individually, one-on-one, through their first few promotions. You even set up the first promotion together. Leave nothing to chance. This is a critical step because it helps the manager get past their initial discomfort in setting up these types of programs. Once they experience how easy it is, you have a much better chance of getting them fully involved in the program.

### Step Five:
### Weekly Support

Once a week, you have an individual telephone training session with each participant. In that phone session, you review what happened the previous week. If there were glitches, you help them work on them. Then you help them set specific goals for the next week. In this way, you'll know weekly if the programs are getting done. Immediately follow up the telephone session with a memo or email summarizing the conversation. Send it to the participant, the supervisor, and as many people up the chain of command that want to keep an eye on the program. It's these summaries that will become the bulk of your fully customized version of the program when you're ready to roll it out system-wide.

### Step Six:
### Monthly Review, Revise, and Recharge (R3)
### Group Sessions

Monthly, you bring the local participants together in their market for a review and advanced No-B.S. Marketer training. This can be done by telephone conference, but it is vastly more effective if the participants can meet in person. My smaller clients generally do this in a monthly meeting at a central location. In these sessions, each participant shares with the rest of the group what they have done and how each promotion worked or didn't work. We find that this process accelerates the program because peers are sharing success stories, and it creates enthusiasm for the program. It also puts subtle pressure on those who are lackluster in their efforts. You serve more as a facilitator in these sessions.

Immediately after these group training sessions, compose your follow-up memo or email summarizing the activity and issues. Send it to all the participants and supervisors.

Ideally, you want to continue on this course for six to nine months. For smaller companies, you begin your step-down period (go directly to Step Seven on page 80). For larger companies, you start preparing for a rollout phase toward the end of this developmental phase. Once you've collected enough tactical stats, samples, and stories it's time to start the next phase of the program.

As mentioned before, this is the most difficult phase as far as getting implementation and overall results from specific promotions. These developmental groups are being trained in a "generic" version of the program, and it is through their efforts that the program becomes customized for your entire system. The program that is presented in the rollout seminar will be far more effective that the one that was presented nine months earlier because all the ideas were fine-tuned during that first phase. It amazes me when I'm conducting a generic No-B.S. Marketer seminar at a convention, I'll teach one tactic and share a supporting anecdote of a pizza place that used it successfully. An audience member may run a car wash and say, "That's fine for pizzas, but how does that work for me?" As incredible as it may seem, the majority of your managers won't be able run with a given tactic unless it is presented totally step-by-step specifically for them.

Also during the development phase, you'll collect numerous samples of printed pieces that were used in the promotions. These certificates, coupons, fliers, danglers, shelf talkers, mailers, and so on were produced for each specific promotion. From these, you will then create easily customizable templates for all other future participants. Some clients keep the templates on file through their local quick printing service so the manager or owner can easily go online, add their contact information, adjust the offer and disclaimers, and have them printed and delivered.

In addition to local implementation of the various promotions, it's usually beneficial to allow your unit mangers to order their own printed matter from their local vendor. Of course you will want to use preapproved templates or ad slicks to ensure that they are following your programs. But your local managers need the agility and speed of arranging for their promotional pieces locally. If you force them to deal with a centralized service, either externally or internally, it will frustrate them and the program will be in jeopardy of falling apart. The additional cost of printing at a local facility is so minimal that it's not worth taking the risk.

### Step Seven:
### Step-Down Phase

Once you're comfortable that your participants are regularly implementing their No-B.S. Marketer tactics, you begin to wean them off of the weekly calls and monthly meetings. Over the next three months, you *gradually* reduce your coaching to one phone call a month and one meeting every three to four months. At that point you'll begin *maintenance mode*. The step-down process begins as you start your Phase II. Step down is important to maintaining the program. If you stop "cold turkey" you stand a chance of losing all the momentum you've built in the previous six to nine months of your program.

I suggest that you first go from weekly phone calls to one call every two weeks and one meeting every other month. After three months of that, you'll then reduce them to one call every three weeks and one meeting every three months. Then, finally, call once a month and have a group meeting once every four to six months. This will be your maintenance level, and you stay with this forever.

Also, your developmental markets will begin to provide you some advanced tactics that only happen in the more mature grassroots marketing units. These improvements, modifications, and innovations can only happen if you keep the program going in the original developmental markets. Then this provides you much of the new material that you'll use in all the other markets after the rollout phase.

We know from experience that not everyone is going to do well in this first phase. Keep in mind that in the development phase, you're taking generic tactics. So it's going to be more difficult to show results than it will in Phase II, where all the ideas have been fleshed out. Therefore, if you need, let's say, 25 units for six months to develop your program properly, you'll actually start with 10 percent more, or 28. You usually can't tell prior to beginning who is going to be a superstar and who a super pain in the rear. But you'll discover it within the first few weeks. There will also be the natural attrition that happens when employees move or quit; don't make a big deal of it. You simply become less proactive for those two or three that will obviously waste your time. And should every single participant call you weekly when scheduled and do their homework, you'll have a more developed program. What you can't afford is to start with the bare minimum and lose several of your managers.

## Phase II

Phase II is only for larger organizations. Smaller businesses can go directly to the next chapter.

### *Rewrite*

While still keeping the pressure up on your developmental markets, you begin the next phase of your program. Taking the promotions that were done by the developmental markets, the No-B.S. Marketer seminar leader will create a new participant manual, presentation outline, and audiovisuals. Don't spend a lot of money making the manual beautiful. And don't let your advertising agency produce it for you. With any luck, it will be obsolete within six months. This is because we assume you'll have numerous improvements and innovations to share for future managers. For that reason we suggest you create a three-ring binder that allows each past participant to update their manual as new ideas and approaches are discovered.

### *Rollout Process*

With the new presentation materials, you start to plan your rollout process. This process, in some respects, will follow the way a new product or procedure is rolled out. You'll choose some key markets to start with. You want markets that are already reasonably successful. You'll save your worst markets for a little later, when you're better equipped to turn them around.

Unlike introducing a new product through a national advertising campaign, you can roll out your No-B.S. Marketer local-level marketing program on a slower, more methodical basis. Pick your rollout markets carefully. You'll include all the units within that market, but you can be selective in assigning weekly phone calls to only those units that are really going to support the program.

The number of units a No-B.S. Marketer Trainer can handle during the rollout phase will depend on several factors. The key factor is the concentration of units in a marketplace. Since you'll have to conduct a monthly meeting with all the participants, you'll want to choose locations within a reasonable commute for a number of unit managers or owners. Generally, a three-hour drive or less works well, though we have had areas where managers came longer distances. If your participants are scattered all over the place it's more difficult. We have done some of the meetings in those situations by conference call or in a webinar format, but they don't have the same power as the in-person meeting.

Next, you will consider the total number of participants. Each participant requires a 10- to 15-minute phone call per week. Not all of them will call you when they're supposed to, and you'll have to become proactive in reaching them, which takes more time. After you have determined your participant number, you write your summary memo, which takes another 5 to 10 minutes.

Once you start the step-down portion of the rollout in a given market, you'll find that you have more time available to start a new market. You may be tempted (or get pressured from your bosses) to speed up this process, but it will trade off some of the maximum benefit from the program. With enough trainers you can conduct an effective rollout in a 12- to 18-month period.

## Turnarounds

When the bulk of your units are in maintenance, or starting their step-down process, you now focus on the problem units. Before investing your valuable resources in these financially challenged units, it helps to first determine the reason why they are underperforming.

Marketing, advertising, and promotion can't help a poorly managed unit. It can't help a unit that is in poor repair. So it's advised that you correct these operational and managerial problems before instituting the No-B.S. Grassroots Marketer program.

Assuming there are no operational reasons why this unit is an underachiever, you're now ready to resuscitate it. It's likely that the unit has a poor reputation in the marketplace, even though the problems have been fixed. So for these units, you'll conduct a more intensive series of promotions designed to put it on the map fast. Again, these tactics are discussed in Chapter 6. But the process you use to install your No-B.S. Marketer program is similar to the rollout; however, it is more intensive.

## Maintenance Phase

This final phase is critical and most often forgotten. Without some consistent effort to reinforce the program, it's too easy for store managers to lapse into old habits and let all that hard work go for naught. It doesn't take a lot to maintain the program. There should be some kind of live event once a quarter. That could be a phone call, conference call, group meeting in a specific market, or a regional or national "Grassroots Marketing" convention. Plus you want to supplement the live events with other reinforcements like a newsletter, e-zine, emails, video updates on the company website, and so on.

Recognition for a manager or owner's efforts is also important. When your organization starts rewarding local-level marketing programs, the unit managers will understand how important their efforts are to the company. For maximum motivation, in addition to presenting awards for successes, make awards part of their bonus program.

### *Special Forces*

Your last step is to address the special needs of the different units. You need a "what if" program in place. Some of these include:

- Grand opening of a new store
- Remodeling
- Competitive intrusion
- Competitive exit
- Manager change
- Access barriers, such as a road-widening in front of the store

### *Replacement*

You need a way to train new managers. Either through expansion or attrition, you will lose some of your trained No-B.S. Marketers.

New ones will take their place. So part of your maintenance program is to bring the new managers online. You could have No-B.S. Marketer training as part of their standard operations training.

One other thing you'll want to explore is building your No-B.S. Marketer team. To do all this stuff, you'll need enough of the right people to make it happen. Of course, this depends on the size of your organization. Keep in mind that as the program grows, so does the cost. Each person you add to your staff who exclusively works on No-B.S. Marketer programs requires that you show an increase in sales to justify it. Work smarter, not harder. Keep your team lean and mean. After all, they're No-B.S. Marketers!

# CHAPTER 6

# Getting Your Hands Dirty
## Neighborhood Marketing Tactics

Jeff Slutsky

With your No-B.S. Marketer neighborhood marketing infrastructure in place, you're ready to start making some tactical headway. Obviously, not every tactic is good for every business or situation. In this chapter you will learn a variety of No-B.S. Marketer tactics. If one of these tactics, at first, doesn't seem to apply to your situation, try to adapt, modify, enhance, or otherwise tweak it. Sometimes the most successful promotions are adaptations from other ideas that, on the surface, didn't seem to apply. As a No-B.S. Marketer, you learn how to identify successful ideas used elsewhere and then make them work for you.

In some respects the tactics presented here are like a wedding: something old, something new, something borrowed, and something blue. If it works, it's included.

## Business Card Handshake

During an 11-week period, the manager of a convenience store passed out 200 of her business cards to people she did not recognize as being her customers. She made a goal of handing out at least 10 a day, and as she set about this, on the back of her business card she would write, "free regular soft drink or coffee" and sign it. Then she would tell the prospective customer, "When you come into our store, the drink's on me!" Of the 200 she passed out, 51 came back; that's over a 25% return. Obviously, most of those who came in and redeemed that card bought other things. Plus, many of those customers came back for more visits.

The unique thing about a business-card handshake promotion is that is has a strong redemption rate and a strong conversion rate. The reason is that it allows you to develop a personal relationship with potential customers. There's a nice ego boost when a customer knows the manager or owner of a business. It makes them feel special. Take advantage of this.

And don't create special "free cards" for this purpose. To really make the person feel special, you use your business card. Handwrite the offer on the back and sign it. That will have a much greater impact for you. We often suggest to our clients that they pass out from 10 to 15 per week. But it's not just handing them out. It's that 15-second greeting that goes along with it. Here's one that worked really well for a popular Tex-Mex franchise:

> "My name is _____, the General Manger at the _____ (*offer your location*). (*Shake hands.*) Have you ever been there before? Do you like burritos? Well, you're going to like ours. Why don't you come on in and be my guest. (*Take out a business card and write offer on back.*) Have a free entree on me. Hope to see you."

## Hindsight Promotion

A very successful stock broker on the East Coast used a different version of business card distribution according to Murray Raphael, author of *The Great Brain Robbery*. While commuting to work, this stockbroker would have to pay several tolls. Before he would pay his tolls, he would first look in his rearview mirror. If he saw an upscale car, he not only would pay his toll but also that of the person in the luxury car behind him. He then asked the toll booth attendant to hand his business card to the person in the car behind him after writing a brief note on the back of the card. The note read, "If you think this is an interesting way of getting your attention, think of all the things I could do for your financial portfolio." He got many new clients off of a simple 90¢ toll and a clever use of his business card.

## The Business Card Drawing

When we're brought into an organization to develop and help implement a No-B.S. Marketer neighborhood marketing program, the first tactic participating managers do is the simple business card drawing. In the hands of a No-B.S. Marketer, this simple tactic provides you several key pieces of information that you'll use in executing many of your promotions over the following 6 to 12 months.

This business card drawing helps you conduct a little bit of reconnaissance about your marketplace so you will get maximum return on your efforts. Knowing in what part of town your customers live and work can be a real advantage when developing special promotions. Or more to the point, knowing what areas of your neighborhood don't seem to patronize you is equally as important.

No doubt you've seen businesses set out fishbowls for dropping in your business card for a free drawing of some prize. You'll do the same, but you're going to use the promotion for more than just creating a mailing list. On the poster above the fishbowl, specifically make the drawing a "business card" drawing. You don't provide entry forms. The reason is that the business card provides you information you want later. Plus, for this promotion you want to gather the names of businesspeople who happen to be your customers. Of course, if you have a customer that doesn't have a business card and wants to participate in the drawing, you can have them put their name and address on a piece of paper or on the back of your card. The prize you select for your free drawing should be just valuable enough to motivate your customers to enter. You don't want it to be so valuable that people want to "stuff" your fishbowl. Also mention on the contest sign that "runner-up prizes will also be awarded."

## *Push-Pin Chart*

After several weeks, you'll draw a winner and give away your prize. Now you have a fishbowl full of business cards. The information on these cards is invaluable. First, they tell you where your customers work. So your first task is to do a *scattergram*, which is a street map of your trade area around your business. Plot the address on the map with pins with colored heads. Once you start plotting enough of your customers on the map, you begin to get a picture of where your customers live and work. You might be pleasantly surprised where you get business.

Now that you have your map plotted, you can take a step back and see exactly where your customers work. With this information you can plan an attack for those geographical areas where you have a weak concentration. For example, if the reason a certain area draws few customers is because there is a park or a lake located there, then you know nothing can be done. However, if on the other hand the map shows you a very weak pull from an area where you have stiff competition, you'll want to attack that area with aggressive promotional offers.

The scattergram can also be used to plot home addresses; however, for that piece of recon you need to provide entry forms and ask for home addresses. Do not run both drawings at the same time.

A scattergram can also be useful to help you select local advertising media. Brad Baker of Bradford W. Baker, a media buying service in Jacksonville, Florida (www.BradfordWBaker. com) uses the scattergram to determine in which local newspapers to buy ad space in for his clients. When the daily newspaper has too broad of a reach (and therefore is too expensive) for a given local businessperson, there are suburban and other weekly publications that may do the job. Brad uses the information from a scattergram to determine geographically which publications reach the customers.

## The Database

The obvious benefit, as mentioned before, is using the information you gathered to build your database. You can use the addresses for mailings and the phone number for calling. Since they're already your existing customers, you can ask them if they would like to get on your "hot list." So when you have special offers, you can give them prior notice of it before your ad breaks in the newspaper.

## Cross-Promotion Partner Leads

The biggest challenge in neighborhood marketing is having the time to meet with other area merchants and set up the various cross promotions. Over the years, this was the one big drawback to getting the ideas implemented. I was challenged by a client—a major quick-oil-change franchisor—to come up with a way that an overworked store manager could get the opportunity to set up these promotions, even given the demands already on his time. The answer was sitting in the waiting room.

I was working with one of several managers in the development phase of their West Coast program. I noticed a gentleman in a very nice suit reading a four-month-old copy of *Time* while waiting for his car. We started chatting. It turned out that he was a recent transfer to the area and headed HR for the John Deere distribution center about a mile down the road. This was his second visit to the shop, after bringing his wife's car the week before. He was really pleased with the quality of service on his cars. I asked him if he would like to provide his 300 employees a new benefit program at no cost to his company. This got his attention.

I then offered to provide special VIP cards that allowed all his employees to receive a 10% discount on any oil change for a three-month period. The only caveat was that the piece had to be inserted in the payroll envelope to ensure that every employee received one. The VIP cards would be printed specifically for them and have the John Deere name on the card. He thought this was a great idea and the promotion was executed.

I and my staff had been teaching our participants how to set up these types of promotions for years, but this one was different. The promotion was set up on-site. I did not have to go knocking on any doors. The time savings was enormous. Plus, the decision maker in this case is already a customer. He needed no introduction to the business, so he was predisposed to working with my client.

That's where your business-card drawing comes in. These cards tell you the names of the companies and titles of the people who are already your customers. Like the John Deere example, you can likely set up your first 20 or 30 promotions with your own customers. Your customer database is your secret weapon to making this work for you.

The more you know about your own customers, the more opportunities you'll have to promote. Business-card drawing aside, you'll also use this approach to develop nonprofit fundraising opportunities, as well, which are designed to bring customers into your location. Starting with your own customer base as a means to create your community outreach program is the key to success.

## Merchant Cross Promotion

The VIP card idea is just one type of cross promotion. That particular approach is used when networking with major employers, education institutions, and associations in your community. A similar promotion, but executed a little differently, is designed to network with other area merchants. It's the merchant cross promotion.

### *Food and Flicks*

The general manager of a Moe's Southwest Grill in Summerville, North Carolina, approached the manager of his local bank branch of BB&T. The bank manager is one of his regulars, so he says, "I've got this idea I want to run by you. For one week, your customers can receive a special certificate worth $5.00 on any purchase at Moe's, as a way of showing BB&T's appreciation for its customers." How could the BB&T branch manager say "No," when everyone benefits?

In just the first few weeks of the promotion, that Moe's generated 226 new customers. To determine if a customer was a first-timer, the cashier at Moe's asked each customer with the certificate if it was the first time to this Moe's. If they said "Yes" the cashier then circled a little "Y" printed on the lower right-hand corner of the certificate. This simple question helped to determine a new customer from one that was a regular. That number will no doubt increase over the weeks following. A few weeks later, the Moe's GM did the same promotion with a local Staples store during a statewide tax-free promotion. That one generated 128 new customers. In less than five months that restaurant received 1,038 new customers from 32 different cross promotions.

In most instances, the GM already knew the cross-promotion partner, most of whom were his customers. The No-B.S. Marketer solution here is that the GM set up this promotion in several minutes and without leaving the store. It not only showed a tremendous return on his investment in money, but also in his time. The business card drawing helps you determine more of these types of opportunities. However, if you can jot down the names of customers that you already know and who would make ideal cross-promotion partners for you, start there.

If you don't want to wait for those key customers to come in, use the phone number on the business card and invite them in. Tell them that you had your drawing and they won the runner-up prize. Set a specific time for the customer to come and to pick it up or ask when he or she plans on visiting again, so you can make sure the prize is ready. That's when you suggest your idea for a promotion.

You shouldn't have to leave your unit to set up a number of promotions over time, as mentioned before. However, there are times when the ROI of a promotion can be potentially so huge that you want to take the time to reach out to possible cross-promotion partners.

Such was the situation with Jason, the manager of a Midwest comic book store. His product, unlike burgers or video rentals, appeals to a very small percentage of the marketplace. Finding a cross-promotion partner that would be worth his effort was not easy, until the release of the *Batman* sequel. Jason reasoned that not everyone who goes to this movie buys comic books, but just about everyone who buys comic books is going to go to this movie. There are not very many venues where he could potentially reach nearly 100% of his potential buyers.

So he set up a promotion with a movie theater during the release of *Batman Returns*. With each ticket sold, the movie-goer got a certificate for $1 off the purchase of any $10 of Batman products. The movie theater handed out 10,000 certificates. The raw exposure alone would have made it worthwhile, yet they got 150 redemptions. Out of those, 50 became regular customers spending an average of $10 per week in his store. It generated about $26,000 of yearly revenue on a one-time $100 promotion! That was certainly worth the extra effort. Plus, once the relationship is established, Jason could return for the release of other similar title-specific opportunities including Superman, Spiderman, X-Men, The Fantastic Four, The Punisher, Catwoman, and so on.

To be fair, not all cross promotions have this dramatic a result. Still, when done right, why does this type of cross-promotion offer such a high return on investment? To understand this, let's look at the "Three I's of No B.S. Grassroots Marketing":

1. Investment
2. Influence
3. Integrity

## *Investment*

The most expensive thing about any advertising is the cost of getting your message distributed to your potential customers. When you buy radio, you pay for the number of people listening. When you buy newspaper, you pay for the number of people reading. With a cross-promotion, on the other hand, you get free distribution of your advertising message. Even the cost of production is minimal. You don't have to use full color and special papers. Simple black ink on standard color paper stock works fine at your local quick printer.

## *Influence*

With a cross promotion you get the same controls as you would with direct mail. You can target geographically and demographically to reach just the people you want to reach. In Jason's situation, he figured those people who went to a movie based on a comic book character would be an ideal group with which to promote. And he was right.

There's one other interesting play with "geographic control." If, after completing your scattergram, you discover that you have weak pull from an area due to a major competitor, you can plan some surgical attacks. Set up promotions specifically around that competitor, ideally further away from you. You'll probably have to use a stronger offer or deeper discount to pull them to you because those customers are further away and there is a competitor between you. You will probably get less return than usual, but the customers you do pull are more likely to be new and you are keeping them away from that competitor.

Geographic control also means that you think very carefully with whom you cross-promote in relation to their distance from your business. One of our earlier efforts involved a Minit Lube manager who set up a cross promotion with the Dairy Queen right next door. People came in to get their oil changed, and since they had a few minutes to kill, the reader board on the Dairy Queen advertising "99¢ Peanut Buster Parfaits" was just too tempting. Many took advantage of the offer. Upon their purchase they were pleasantly surprised to be awarded a $2.00-off certificate redeemable at the Minit Lube next door. How fortuitous it was! When they got their bill after the oil change, they presented their $2.00-off certificate.

**FIGURE 6.1:** Cross-Promotional Offers too Close to Your Location

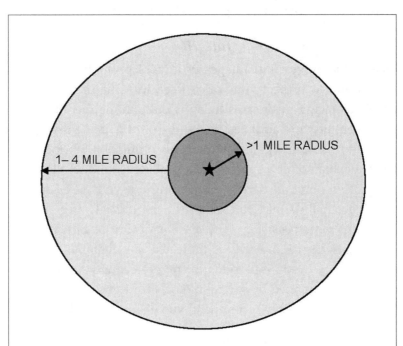

Figure 6.1 shows how aggressive cross-promotional offers too close to your location can cannibalize your regular sales. There's nothing for you in the doughnut hole!

The quick-lube place got several dozen redemptions. But the ROI was negative. The way this promotion was executed, it only ended up discounting people who were going to pay full price anyway. No new customers resulted from this promotion. If you have a new business and not a great deal of awareness in your community, cross-promoting in your back yard may make sense. For a more mature store or business, you want to think of a "doughnut" shape (see Figure 6.1). Place your store in the middle of the doughnut hole, which may create a two- or three-block radius. Stores in that circle are too close. Then, you have the doughnut from beyond the hole to about three or four miles out. That's where you place your efforts from a geographical point of view.

## *Integrity*

One of the biggest advantages of a cross promotion is that it allows you to protect your price integrity. One of the biggest problems facing businesses today is discounting, because your customers become addicted to the discount and then refuse to pay full price ever again. With a cross promotion, on the other hand, you can offer a special savings of some kind, but because the cross-promotion partner is handing out your offer and on their behalf, they take full credit for the special offer. You've *transferred the responsibility of the discount to the other merchant* and your regular price integrity is protected. Incidentally, the most complete how-to-do-it presentation on protecting your price and profit is championed by my co-author, Dan Kennedy, in *No B.S. Price Strategy*. I highly recommend you get it and read it!

## *Setting Up the Promotion*

So how to you get another merchant to be willing to hand out your advertising for you, free of charge? You have to approach them properly. Here's an example of what I might say:

> My name is Jeff Slutsky with Jeff's Flower Shop down the street. I saw a program that worked for someone else and I wanted to run it by you. [*Show a sample of the other promotion.*] I would like to offer you the opportunity of providing your customers something extra, a way you can give them a little bit more for their money and a great way for you to personally thank them for being your customers. What do you think?

At this point you wait for them to come back with something like, "Well, it sounds great, but how much is this going to cost?" This response usually happens about 99 out of 100 times. So you respond with, "Well, let me ask you this: If it were free, would you do it?" Then they'll say something like, "Free? Sure, why not?" You then simply respond with, "Fair enough!" and the promotion is a done deal. Before you leave, get their weekly customer count so you know how many pieces to print. Be sure to get a couple of copies of their logo so you can print it right on the certificate. Also check the correct spelling of their name, or even a signature to put on the piece. In this way, the top of the certificate will read, "This special thank you is compliments of (Logo) and (Signature), Owner (or Manager)." By including both the merchant's name and the owner or manager's name, you transfer responsibility twice, and that person has a very personal reason for making sure all of the pieces get distributed to customers.

To get a little practice in, set up your first few promotions with good friends of yours. They don't have to be high-priority cross-promotion partners because the purpose of these promotions is to give you practice setting them up and getting the materials printed and delivered.

### The Reverse Cross Promotion

A jewelry store located in a mall in Indiana competed with a dozen or more others in their marketplace. The challenge was to create some kind of cost-effective value-added motivator for shoppers to commit to his engagement rings instead of going repeatedly to all the other stores. The No-B.S. Grassroots Marketing was the "wedding package."

The manager went to his friends who also served the wedding market. He asked them what it would be worth to them to have access to people in the market for wedding services at the point when they first decide to get married. Of course it was a loaded question. The first step on the marriage go-round is the engagement ring. This manager had access to a group of customers that other businesses find very valuable. But instead of asking these businesses to buy advertising to reach this group, he wanted an exclusive offer from their business. He asked for something of significant value (either discount or value added) to the couple but also made sense to the vendors if they got advance access to potential wedding business.

The jewelry store manager created a packet of offers. The envelope and inserts had the same look and feel of a nice wedding invitation. But inside there were a dozen pieces that had exclusive offers from the bakery, the bridal shop, the tux shop, the photographer, limousine service, banquet hall, travel agency, florist, invitation printer, dance studio, and weight loss. The pieces were printed for free by the invitation printer who received placement on the top of the packet for that additional contribution.

The value of this package was over $1,000, with a mix of some discounts and some freebies. Now, when a happy couple first looks for an engagement ring but wants to continue looking because it's several hundred dollars more than they wanted to spend, he has a sweetener: If you go with this ring today, we have this special wedding packet that is worth over $1,000 in savings on your wedding. It made a great closing tool, and the cost was nothing to him. This has a much higher perceived value than a $200 discount and is much more profitable. Plus, many of the other merchants participating in the wedding packet agreed to use his cross-promotion piece with their customers later in the year.

### *Nonmerchants*

It's not just retailers who can use these types of ideas. With a little massaging and tweaking you can make them work in a variety of situations. Consider Edye, a drug representative for a major pharmaceutical company. Her job depends on getting access to busy doctors to make a five-minute presentation (called detailing) about a specific medication. There was a time when the company provided spiffs and freebies to help them gain access to the doctors, but times changed and that was taken from the budget.

Edye knew that about half of her 400 doctors played golf. With no budget to buy golf items, her No-B.S. Marketer solution was to approach a retail chain of golf equipment stores in town. She asked the regional manager: How valuable would it be to get several hundred doctors to visit one of their area stores? The regional manager knew that a doctor represented a couple thousand dollars of sales over an 18-month period (he obviously did the exercise to determine the value of a new customer).

Edye suggested that he give her 200 certificates good for a box of free Titlist golf balls. This was a retail value then of about $25.00. His cost was around $10.00. She then used the gift certificates that had an expiration date of only two weeks to give to her doctors. And many of them actually drove across town to redeem their certificate. To be valid, Edye had to present the certificate in person, and it had to be signed by the doctor. She was able to get face-to-face with more doctors and the golf store chain got many new customers for very little money.

She also used the same idea to gain favor with the receptionists and nurses in the doctors' offices. These people are the gatekeepers, and the better her relationship with them, the more effectively she could do her job. A manicurist was just starting out at a local hair salon and had more time than money to promote her new venture. Edye suggested that she give her 100 certificates for free manicures. Many of the nurses who would redeem these might end up being repeat customers; plus, even though the manicure would be free, she still would get some tips. Edye was able to get a couple of thousand dollars' worth of free manicures, which made her very popular among the staff. And the fledgling manicurist got her business off the ground in less than a month.

What cross-promotion partners would you want to pursue? Think in terms of what businesses or organizations people would seek when going through a given life change. What kind of added value could you provide to make it worth the effort to refer you to them? What is the potential ROI from such an effort done right?

### *Seasonal Promotions*

Not all businesses see their customers equally throughout the year. For example, to get the most exposure from cross-promoting with a card shop, florist, jewelry store, candy store, and photo finishing store, you might want to consider setting up your promotions before Valentine's Day, Easter, Mother's Day, and Christmas. (You may want to add Sweetest Day.) If you want more exposure toward the beginning of the New Year, cross-promote with businesses that have to do with New Year's resolutions, including health clubs, weight loss, and smoking cessation. Early April you'll get a lot of action from lawn and garden services, mulch suppliers, tanning salons, and tax preparers. You need to pick up business in late October? Cross-promote with a costume shop. They have one big season during the year and it's the week before Halloween.

The difference in your ROI from doing a cross promotion any time, or at the right time, for a given type of partner can be 10 to 20 times more. Think three months ahead in your planning so you identify who and when you want to promote to maximize your efforts and your return on marketing investment. The table in Figure 6.2 lists half the year's seasonal opportunities to keep in mind.

FIGURE **6.2:** Look for Special Tie-Ins to Events on Your Calendar

| | |
|---|---|
| 1-Jan | New Year's Day |
| 17-Jan | Martin Luther King Day |
| 1-Feb | National Freedom Day |
| 2-Feb | Groundhog Day |
| 3-Feb | Chinese New Year |
| 14-Feb | Valentine's Day |
| 21-Feb | Presidents' Day |
| 8-Mar | Mardi Gras |
| 13-Mar | Daylight Saving Time begins |
| 17-Mar | St. Patrick's Day |
| 15-Apr | Tax Day |
| 24-Apr | Easter Sunday |
| 27-Apr | Administrative Professionals Day |
| 5-May | Cinco de Mayo |
| 8-May | Mother's Day |
| 21-May | Armed Forces Day |
| 30-May | Memorial Day |

## *In the Loop Promotion*

Sometimes you get more by helping your competitor. That may sound strange, but there are special situations where promoting your competitor will help increase your sales. One example of this is the "in the loop" promotion. The first time I used this type of promotion was when I was part owner of a nightclub. Most of our customers, even the "regulars," did a certain amount of bar hopping. We knew our club was one of perhaps 20 that they could visit in a given night.

The idea behind "in the loop" was to create an association of nightclub owners with whom we had a good relationship. There were six of us in all. We had a special certificate created that was given to our customers when they left our club. The other five establishments would do the same. The offer on the promotional piece was good at any of the other five operations for that night. This would provide an incentive for those customers, leaving to go elsewhere, to choose one of the nightclubs in the loop. So as customers around town started to bar hop, once they hopped into one of our six participants, our group would capture that customer and keep them in our loop.

Each club owner could track the results because the customer was redeeming a certificate. Once a customer went to any of the six participating "loop" clubs, there were incentives to keep them in the loop. Therefore, the market share of the six increased, as did their sales.

A more recent example of this came up when a regional fast-food hamburger restaurant, the top franchisee in the chain, found out a new competitor was moving into the market. This hamburger place competes toe-to-toe with a national hamburger franchise down the street. The national hamburger franchise, like the regional competitor, is on the short list of one of the highest volume units in the chain.

Now they both face competition from a new player. How can they work together? Here are a few of the suggestions given to them:

- During the week leading up to the new competitor's grand opening, the two old competitors hand out certificates to their customers promoting the other's restaurant. The purpose is to keep people from trying the new place.
- Shut down for one lunch day part (shift). That's right, shut down. Then put up a banner that says, "In honor of our

new neighbor, we're closed. Go visit them." With both high-volume places shut down, the only place to go will be the new place. And since it's likely they aren't expecting to have 100% of the market share that lunch, customers will probably be waiting a very long time for their food. They will get annoyed at the slow service, and food items will likely sell out. They'll get angry. And, since their first experience with this new competitor is likely to be negative, they may vow never to return.

I think you'll find now that there are a number of different ways to get your advertising distributed free. But more than getting your advertising out there without costing you, when you structure these promotions properly, they do much more. It's a one-on-one type of communication that has more credibility than mass media. You're not only getting exposure for free but a testimonial from your cross-promotion partner. When you start thinking of all the people you know in your community, you'll begin to see just how these relationships can boost your business. The graphic in Figure 6.3 on page 106 will help you get started working with them.

**FIGURE 6.3:** Sample of Relationships for Community-Based Marketing

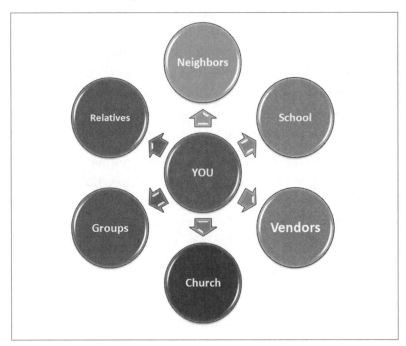

# CHAPTER 7

# Rethinking the Business
## You Are In

Dan Kennedy

T ip O'Neill famously said, "All politics is local."
That was in the Reagan era, when Tip and Ronald Reagan
were already old war horses. Surely it can't still be a
truism in today's world of social media and online community, a
more complex media landscape with so many more options, and
a more mobile society, can it? Today, Congress has the lowest
favorable ratings in the polls ever, and the "throw the bums out"
fervor is high, yet most incumbents get re-elected. How can that
be? Because everybody else's Congressman is a bum, but my guy
answers my mail, got the money to fix a bridge and build a public
swimming pool, kept a military base from getting closed during
Pentagon budget cuts, and is at every local parade, county fair,
rib cook-off, and is just an all-around good guy.

In the very early stage of the 2012 presidential campaign, a candidate on the Republican side, who appeared to have a chance of at least being competitive in the primaries, suffered an amazing campaign collapse when his entire staff quit on the same day. Lots of candidates fire campaign managers and even entire staffs, but nobody can recall an entire staff firing a candidate. Their chief reasons: that he was proving utterly undisciplined and refusing to do any of the real work of political campaigning: calling and speaking to donors personally, getting out to diners and community events, doing living room meetings, pressing the flesh. He believed he could replace all that with new media. His campaign experts, as young as 30-ish, believed otherwise. One of the most famous masterminds of online and social media for politics, who had advised Howard Dean, and then Barack Obama, commented that all the new media is obviously powerful, but none of it can replace a handshake, a look straight in someone's eye, a direct answer to a personal question.

We might add to Tip's admonition that all politics is also *personal*. In the early presidential primary contests, there are caucuses and straw polls, not just elections. Participation is small, made up mostly of party faithful, passionate activists, and donors. In many cases, as incredible as it may seem in this age of technology, social media, and proliferate advertising media, the successful candidate will have met every voter in person, some often enough to actually know them by name. But even in the bigger arena, professional politicians master the making of it all personal. As a speaker, I appeared on about a dozen seminar events with former President George H. W. Bush and wife Barbara Bush. At the first one, I met and very briefly chatted with President Bush backstage. Well over a month later, I encountered him backstage again, and he asked how my books were doing, how my horse-racing was going, and what I thought about an advertising-related news item of the week. There was no reason for him to have bothered to remember me at all, let alone remember details of my business and personal activities. I later asked Barbara Bush about it and she explained that (a) George had trained himself to have an amazing memory for just such information, but (b) that he also cheated, creating notes about everybody he met, that he could use to freshen memory in advance if he knew he was about to encounter that person again, or refer to in correspondence because (c) that was actually what a political career and influence was all about, and—with a twinkle in her eye—(d) you just never knew when it would come in handy, soliciting donations for the next son to run for president or some charitable cause.

This gets us, long-windedly and circuitously, to the core question, the multimillion-dollar question of what business you are really in. This will back us up two chapters, as the last two chapters by Jeff have been about re-organizing your thinking, strategies, tactics, actions, and behavior for a different business than you likely thought you were in when you first picked up this book. Most businesspeople confuse their deliverables with the business they are in. If they own a restaurant, they think they are in the food service business or food plus entertainment business, but that's like George H. Bush thinking he was in the governance business. He knew his deliverable when in office was governance, but his business was list-building, relationship building, influence, and fund-raising, all dependent on "local" and "personal." A lot of No-B.S. Marketers advance from confusing the business they're in with its deliverables to thinking of themselves as professional marketers in the marketing business, then a marketer of a restaurant, or veterinary practice, or whatever, and that *is* advancement. But the No-B.S. Grassroots Marketer goes another few steps further. He uses marketing and marketing prowess in ways that create one-on-one relationships at the local level, directly if his business is local, or if his business is regional or national, by making each of its offices, stores, or outposts act as a local business.

For a time, for about two years, I did a lot of consulting with an international conglomerate-owned health products company, with over 1,000 franchised offices across the country. Many were in the hands of multi-unit, territorial franchise owners, who then had hired managers at each location. The franchise owners themselves were distanced from any one office and its community, and, of course, the corporate leaders were even further distanced. Other offices had franchise owner-operators, with the office's owner actually in it, and living in its community. The most successful, most profitable offices achieving top performance in every meaningful statistic, and most importantly, top performance in client-to-client referrals, were owner-operated in relatively small sized markets, and on investigation, it became obvious that these owner-operators were not relying on the corporate brand advertising or on their own local media advertising; they were true grassroots marketers, out and about and active in their communities. In fact, as I read the first draft of Jeff's Chapter 5, I saw almost a carbon copy of the marketing plan used by these grassroots marketers who owned these offices.

A big part of my advice to this client was to reverse-engineer what these grassroots operators were doing and push it back upstream. Get the hands-off, multi-unit owners to get better trained, better committed, better paid, and incentivized managers to act as if they were single-office, grassroots marketers. This advice incorporated a lot of what you read in Jeff's Chapter 4. Sadly, this particular client was unwilling to restructure their marketing in this manner and even more unwilling to impose it on their franchisees, and they have remained a fragile, vulnerable, troubled company very subject to damage by independent, grassroots competitors in many of their markets, skyrocketing costs associated with mass advertising, competitive pressure from discounters, and other evils.

While I did some of the best work of my life for this client, and some of its franchise owners benefited greatly from it, overall I consider the two-year effort a failure, mostly of will on the client's part, the will to do what was and is really necessary to immunize a business of their type to evolutionary destruction by online, cheaper-price marketers, big box discounters entering the product category, excess dependence on costly mass advertising, and vulnerability to little independents in each locality.

This gets us to another subject: *immunity*. Most people understand that they have a personal, physical, physiological, and psychological immune system they need to keep healthy and strong, to ward off disease, delay adverse effects of aging, and protect their ability to perform. Successful athletes pay more attention to this and exert greater effort and discipline regarding it than most ordinary people do, but you are at least aware of the threats to your immune system, and of most common dangers of a weakened or poorly functioning immune system. Many people, for example, consciously eat green, leafy vegetables and "blue" fruits because of their anti-oxidant and immune system bolstering properties. As cold and flu season approaches, or if you are often surrounded by children, i.e., walking, talking germ factories, you probably take extra vitamin C and zinc. (Note: I'm not dispensing medical advice, just making an observation.) Most businesspeople fail to think of their business as having its own immune system, or of the need and value of keeping their business's immune system healthy and strong, but businesses do have such things, and if they are poorly nourished, inadequately invested in, and permitted to become weak and vulnerable, a lot of very bad things can happen.

The equivalent of a very bad prolonged flu season for a lot of businesses has been the sour economy that fell into recession, affecting just about everybody somewhere around early to mid-2008, and has worsened considerably all the way into the days I'm working on this particular chapter (mid-2011). Businesses with weak immune systems got sick and have stayed sick, and some have died.

One of the keys to the strongest possible business immune system is positive, direct relationships with customers at the local level, nose to nose, face to face, handshake to handshake, being your customer's neighbor in his neighborhood. The little, local, main-street bookstore in a small town adjacent to mine has zero immunity against the bigger selection, ease of ordering, and discounts offered me if simply buy all my books from Amazon, and were I not rich, the recession might very well have added importance to those discounts. Their only immunity is that I like going there, hearing about books they've personally picked and read, being led to the discovery of something I might not have found on my own, and the fact that I identify with this little Main Street and its community, frequently dine at a locally owned eatery a few doors down the street, and buy tailored clothes at a local clothier a few more doors away.

You have to take your immunity against evil forces wherever you can get it.

Jeff has laid out very sensible instruction and examples in the previous two chapters, whether you are actually a local business owner and operator, or heading up a larger entity with a far-flung network of stores, offices, or sales agents. His suggestions are all about getting local and making it personal. They require you to decide that is the business you are in. I urge making that decision.

# CHAPTER 8

# Inside Your Four Walls

Jeff Slutsky

$S$ ome of the best No B.S. Grassroots Marketing is comprised of ideas that can be done on-site. The obvious advantage to these types of promotion is that you have total control over their implementation, since you are not promoting in conjunction with another merchant or organization. Plus, anytime you can arrange a low-cost promotion that does not require you to leave your operation to implement it, you've met one critical condition of a No-B.S. Marketer solution with local-level marketing. Your investment of your time is minimal.

## Employee Contest Solutions

The employee incentive contest is a fail-safe idea that can be done several times a year. It takes very little time to set up and almost always provides a super return. First, create certificates that have a strong offer on your product or service. This offer should be better than any standard coupon or discount that you would use. The actual printed piece can be one-fourth of a piece of paper and works best when printed on colored card stock with one color of ink. This special certificate contains a line at the bottom for your employee's signature and a date.

One of our Street Fighter clients, in Gastonia, North Carolina, received 942 redemptions, of which 250 were first-time buyers from a single crew referral contest promotion. They have a conversion ratio of first-time to regular customer of 27%. That means that of those 250 first-timers, 67.5 will become regular customers valued at about $500 annually. *So for the 12 months following the crew contest, our client will have added $33,750 of additional top-line revenue from a promotion that cost him, at the most, $50.*

Here's how it works: Participation in the contest is totally voluntary. Any full- or part-time employee can participate. You start by giving each participating employee 50 of the certificates. They sign them. Then you explain that, on their own time and beyond the perimeter of your parking lot, they can hand them out. Give them to friends, family, and anybody else they come in contact with, like the postman, the cashier, and so on. Their signature authorizes the special discount.

The contest can run for four weeks. If a given employee runs out of cards, you give them more. The results of the contest are based on redemptions. The employee with the most redemptions each week wins the first-place prize, second most redemptions gets the second-place prize, etc.

You don't have to spend a lot of money on the prizes; most of the time, the managers or owners barter for prizes. They'll collect gift certificates from other area merchants, especially those they've done cross promotions with. These prizes have included video rentals, car washes, restaurant gift certificates, movie passes, free oil changes, CDs, books, small electronics, and so on.

At the end of the month, you tally up all the redemptions and award your grand prize. We've given away items including flat-screen TVs, MP3 players, and Xboxes, but the one prize that had the most impact was the one that cost the least: a day off with pay.

This simple contest is a lot of fun for your crew. They get to provide their friends and acquaintances a really good deal at your business. Of course, you're getting the distribution of that printed piece that provides motivation for that new customer to come in. With 10 employees averaging 50 pieces, you're getting 500 individually distributed certificates. You should find a very strong redemption rate given the unique method of distribution. Additionally, that piece was personally handed out by an employee, adding integrity to the program.

You'll probably find that there's one employee who does way better than everyone else. And it's probably someone you least expect it from. One of the pleasant side effects of this promotion is that you identify an employee who really likes to market. This person can be a valuable resource for other marketing programs, including helping you set up more cross promotions or supervising some of your community involvement activities.

## Customer Referral Program

Every businessperson will tell you that referrals are the best form of advertising. It certainly has the highest ROI since it costs you nothing. But you can't always rely on your customers to aggressively promote you as much as you'd like them to. So give them a little extra incentive to think of you when they are out talking to their friends and acquaintances. When a person first buys a membership in a health club, karate school, yoga class, Lamaze class, dance school, or other self-help activity, that is the magic time when you are most likely to get referrals. You have a window of about two to four weeks, which is the time they're most excited. But instead of leaving their referral effort to chance, make it easy for them.

With each new membership or student signup, the new member is given three referral cards good for one free week or two free classes. The member signs and dates the cards to authorize the free trial program for his or her friend. If the friend signs up for a full membership, the referring member gets a spiff. The health club would add a free month to their membership, while the karate club would give the person $25. The cash seemed to make the bigger impact, but either way can work well. Unlike the employee referral contest, this is an ongoing promotion. If the member uses all three of the "buddy passes" he or she can get more.

The printed certificate is part of the program's success. You don't rely on your member or student or customer to tell their friends to come in for a free class. That printed certificate or pass provides them a tangible reminder of the referral program. When they give one to a friend, now the friend has a tangible reminder. And when that friend redeems the pass, you have a tangible way of tracking the results. Having them tell you "Joe sent me" just won't do the job.

You can even take this ongoing referral program and annually run a more aggressive contest with it, in a similar vein as the employee referral program. Barter prizes, and get a nice grand prize. Put up posters to promote the contest.

With a slight modification, nearly any type of business can use the customer referral program. Our Mercedes salesman offered dinners for two at a very nice restaurant if we gave his card to a friend who would come in for test drive. This guy felt so strongly about the appeal of his product and his ability to sell it that he gave us the spiff just for access to the right people, whether they bought or not. Clothes, jewelry, greeting cards, insurance, and just about any other kind of business could benefit from an organized customer referral program. This is one of those promotions that is a "must have" in any No-B.S. Marketer's war chest of tactics.

## Suggest-Sell Promotions

Suggest selling is a simple and inexpensive marketing technique used at the time of a purchase to increase sales and profitability. It may be as simple as getting your counter people to say, "You want fries with that?" But in the real world it often takes a little more initiative to get your people to suggest that one extra item that is so critical to adding those extra dollars to your bottom line. With the right approach, you'll discover that it is relatively easy to add 10% to 20% more to an existing sale or get an existing customer to buy just one more item.

My all-time favorite example of the suggest-sell contest is the restaurant that, despite having really great banana cream pie, had very weak dessert sales. To motivate his wait staff to suggest dessert more aggressively, the owner ran a contest. For one month, the server who sold the most banana cream pies would win one banana cream pie—to throw it in the owner's face! You never saw such a motivated crew in your life. Just by getting them to suggest dessert, the restaurant's dessert sales increased nearly 50% during the contest. After the contest, the residual effect was a 20% increase in desert sales overall. Think about the return on investment from this one promotion. For the wholesale cost of one banana cream pie, and the dry cleaning of one three-piece suit, he added thousands of dollars to the bottom line each week. And the side effect was that the crew had a great time with it. They didn't feel like they were being pressed to "push" something. They enjoyed it and the customers responded as a result.

An ice cream manufacturer in Canada wanted to promote its product more aggressively through a convenience store chain. They offered to provide to the chain a contest enticing their employees to suggest-sell the ice cream bars at the cash register during a purchase. It was suggested that the ice cream company use a mystery shopper approach where each store would be visited several times during the month. If the employee would suggest-sell an ice cream bar to the mystery shopper, that employee was handed a $50 bill on the spot. If they failed, they were handed a printed note telling them they just lost $50 but they may get another chance. A contest like this creates excitement for employees, and as soon as someone wins some cash, the word spreads.

Suggest selling doesn't have to be limited to food items or contests. A good example from a service business is the approach we use in our own business. Once a client has booked one of us for a sales or marketing seminar for a meeting or convention, our salespeople offer to sell copies of our book, *Street Fighter Marketing*, in quantity for the attendees. When books are purchased as an "add-on" to a speaking contract, the client gets them for less than half of the retail price; this happens about one-third of the time and generally adds about another 50% to that sale. Those clients get a great price for the books, their attendees walk away with something tangible in their hands from the seminar, and we increase our sales.

To apply this to your business, identify a product or service that is high margin, low cost, and has broad appeal. Then, give the customer a reason to buy that extra item on the spot. A hardware store would upsell light bulbs at the counter. The cashier would inform the customer that they're running a special on boxes of four light bulbs; buy one, get the second one half price. About half the customers would take advantage of the offer. The video rental store would do it with two-for-one boxes of candy; the quick-oil-change place, with 25% off air filters.

Once you figure out the item and the offer, you create a fun contest around it. You can use the mystery shopper approach or you can give a prize to the employee with the most items sold. A major department store used a similar approach by giving their employee one giant Hershey bar for each new credit card application they took. A department store credit card usually means that that customer will spend at least 10% more in-store. The cost of the Hershey bars was a mere fraction of the total additional sales generated from each new card holder.

### *Reward Program for Keeping Appointments*

Canceled, no-show, and short-notice changes in appointments can cost professional offices a lot of money. In a dental office, it's estimated that it costs upwards of 30% of annual production according to a leading practice consultant. That could translate to $130,000 of lost revenue in the average practice. So a $10,000 investment could show a significant return if it gets those patients to keep their appointments. That investment was used for a special patient reward program. Here's how it worked:

- The practice started promoting the program to patients six months in advance.
- Each patient must keep two consecutive regular checkup appointments.
- If they cancel, reschedule, or don't show, they are disqualified.
- All eligible patients gather for a year-end party.
- Their bill must be current.
- The patient must follow recommended treatment.
- A drawing is held for the winner of the grand prize at the patient appreciation party.

This is a win/win program for all because the patients receive the care they need and the office generates more productive time in the schedule. Keeping the schedule full not only increases revenue from the regular checkups, but also it gives the doctor an opportunity to diagnose problems that would have otherwise gone untreated. Again, the patient wins because more serious conditions are dealt with earlier, and the office benefits from increased production.

One Midwestern dental office, which was using $5,000 for their grand prize, went from $30,000 to $48,000 in collections, and they're still improving. Even more impressive was the $10,000 grand prize used by an East Coast office that improved from $30,000 to $75,000.

To further enhance the value of the party, additional prizes were donated by other businesses, whose owners just happened to also be patients. Of course, it's hard to turn down a request for a free TV, trip, photography, or use of a time share when the dentist is coming at you with the business end of a big drill.

The program, contest, and appreciation party were promoted with statement stuffers, promotional buttons worn by the staff, and a three-foot-by-six-foot "publisher's clearinghouse" style check on display in the lobby, "paid to the order of our appreciated patient." Also, when patients would call to reschedule they were told they could but it would disqualify them for the grand prize drawing at the patient appreciation party later that year. It was estimated that at least two-thirds of the patients decided they didn't need to change their appointment after all.

Though designed specifically for dental offices, this type of contest could be used for any service business where you're selling time. Examples might include hair salons, massage, chiropractic, optical, cleaning services, lawn care, personal trainer, financial planner, CPA, etc. One interesting comment has been that the patient who won the grand prize often used that money to get more dental work done that was not covered by insurance.

## I'll Show You Mine:
## Reciprocal Displays

This promotion is a little more involved, but under the right circumstances can effectively promote your key products to a strong target audience. Such was the case of the scuba shop that set up a display at a nearby travel agency. They cordoned off a small section near the front of the travel agency that was aggressively promoting cruises with great ports of call for diving and snorkeling. The scuba shop brought their mannequins from their show room, fully dressed in wet suit, tanks, fins, masks, etc. They created a little display with other scuba paraphernalia, and added some signage offering a free scuba lesson to any person signing up for one of their cruises.

That same display at his scuba store was fine for helping to create interest in people already considering scuba. But by moving that display to the travel agency, his exposure increased dramatically to a new group of potential customers.

This approach can be used by any number of businesses: grocery store and appliance store; Domino's and home theater; makeup counter and glamour photography. It's a three-dimensional variation of a cross promotion that can make wonderful impact. Combine it with the distribution of the cross-promotion certificate to ensure that the visual has a take-away piece that helps complete the sale.

Some doctors' and dentists' offices have a tropical fish tank because it helps to relax patients. If you have a pet store, you may want to provide the service of setting up the tanks and maintaining them in exchange for a sign that tells the patients that your business is responsible for this tank. Also include cross-promotion pieces that the office distributes every so often, say, offering a special deal on a starter tank. The same approach might also work for an upscale seafood restaurant.

## Internal Signage

Once someone is at your location, you have a number of different ways to communicate with them that cost very little money and take very little time. Use those opportunities to reinforce why they should buy from you. For example, if your business has a waiting room, provide some reading material that does more to position your business than some out-of-date copies of *U.S. News and World Report*. Testimonial letters or thank-you letters placed in a three-ring binder would make for some interesting reading while at the same time telling your customers how wonderful you are.

If you get some good, positive publicity, have it framed and placed in your waiting area. Or better yet, have it enlarged to poster size. An orthodontist might have a wall filled with patients' photos just after their braces are removed. This "success wall" is a great reinforcement to anyone inquiring about that procedure.

You can also use simple signs to help suggest-sell additional items.

Another form of internal marketing is the "bag stuffer." Place a flier or other type of promotional piece in the customer's bag to help you promote specific items. You can also use the bag stuffer as a form of promotional currency with another business. You place their promotional piece in your bags for your customers in exchange for their promotion of your store.

A really simple message can be delivered by a two-inch button worn by employees. This can reinforce a special item in conjunction with other signs and fliers in your location.

You can really generate some word-of-mouth exposure by doing something totally outrageous from time to time. T. Scott Gross, a professional speaker who came out of the restaurant business, used a technique he calls "random acts of kindness." About once every quarter, without any advance notice, all the meals on that day are free. When the customers came in that day they had no idea it was going to happen. The return on investment is extremely high because the cost of those meals generates so much word-of-mouth exposure that sales instantly increase in the following weeks. You could take that same investment in free meals and place it in advertising and you would likely gain only a fraction of the new business that an innovative, grassroots promotional tactic can generate.

To determine the best form of internal marketing for your business, try to walk into your business with a fresh look. Walk through your front door and imagine what it is like for a first-time visitor. Where is their eye drawn? What does the environment do to make the customers feel comfortable about buying more? How do your people greet that customer? Even if that person is busy helping someone else, they can glance over and acknowledge that the person is there with a nod and perhaps gesture that they'll be with them in just minute. It's a little thing but it makes people feel better about buying from you.

If you've seen magazine or newspaper articles that make the consumers smarter about buying your products and services, and it also helps to reinforce the value you offer, have them enlarged and displayed. Have you won awards? Display the plaque or certificate and then some additional information to explain why winning this award is so significant.

One of the biggest annoyances that your customers have is waiting in line for service. Sometimes this can't be helped. But you want to do everything you can to make that experience less frustrating.

### *Doggy Dog Promotion*

One clever promotion was used by a burger franchisee from their South Carolina unit. He came up with the idea "Dogs eat free." Of course everyone has heard of promotions where kids eat free, but dogs got our attention. They collect the unused hamburgers that normally would have to be thrown out. They cut them up in bite sizes pieces and they give them to the customers' dogs when they go through the drive-thru window. The promotion is done on a specific day of the week, and customers come by regularly to take advantage of the promotion. The really clever part of the promotion is that it costs nothing. They don't have to buy treats since they're using their own product.

## Worst Seat in the House

Brad Kent, in an *Entrepreneur* magazine online article published January 11, 2005, describes one interesting promotion that turned a negative into a positive. The owner of a small café had one of his tables close to the door, and no one ever wanted to sit there. He decided to label the table "the worst table in the house." If you sat there, you'd save 50% on your entire check. Within a week, people in the neighborhood were talking about this café and the table they'd sat at last night where they got their dinner for half price. There were some evenings when people would wait as long as 45 minutes to get that table.

## Neighborhood Blitz

Branch bank managers are generally not the most comfortable in a selling situation. So this one region of Cincinnati-based Fifth-Third banks organized neighborhood blitzes. Two branch managers would team up for several days. On the first day, they would canvass the businesses in the first branch's territory and repeat that the second day for the other branch. They would simply go door to door to small businesses and introduce themselves and hand out a coffee mug with the bank logo on it. When they got the ear of a decision-maker they would try to uncover what potential needs were not being met and see if there was interest in considering their bank.

### Your Inside Job

When you take a look around your business, you'll begin to see many opportunities for communicating with your customers. These opportunities are the least expensive and easiest to execute, so look at your business with fresh eyes.

---

## How Environment Affects Sales and Word-of-Mouth Advertising

### by Dan Kennedy

Far too little attention is paid by most retailers, restaurant owners, and professionals who meet with clients or serve patients in their offices to the impact on the environment, which Jeff touched on in several spots in the just-concluded chapter. My friend Mike Vance, the former dean of Disney University and a celebrated creativity consultant to great companies like Marriott hotels, talks about the five-sensed environment—that people are subconsciously if not consciously affected by input from all five of their senses, not just sight. That's why cookie stores in malls have fans sending the smell of fresh-baked cookies wafting throughout the mall. It's why you should consider what people smell in your place of business. You can learn more about Mike Vance's work at IntellectualEquities.com. His partner, Diane Deacon, conducts seminars, workshops, and trainings; publishes resources; and consults on creative thinking.

---

# How Environment Affects Sales and Word-of-Mouth Advertising

*continued*

In working with financial advisors, I spend a lot of time talking about what potential clients see in their reception rooms and conference rooms. If their clientele is 60+ seniors, then what we call "nostalgia anchors" are important; photos and artifacts they'll have fondness for. There are also "affinity anchors," such as models of U.S. Navy battleships if you are marketing to Navy veterans. In working with chiropractors and dentists, I, like Jeff, urge getting rid of the old magazines and moving in the testimonial books, before/after photo books, and other material to reinforce only these objectives for the patient being there:

1. Get educated;
2. Get interested;
3. Be receptive;
4. Get well faster, i.e. be compliant; and
5. Refer.

One of the grand masters of "'the art of exceptional customer experience" is my co-author of the book *Uncensored Sales Strategies,* Sydney Barrows. Sydney often goes to clients' businesses, sometimes at first as a secret shopper, and then as a "fresh-eyes" consultant, to identify every little thing that may be incongruent with positioning, undermining sales, or retarding referrals, and to create improvements. She works with Sales Choreography® to strategize the optimum physical environment

# How Environment Affects Sales and Word-of-Mouth Advertising

*continued*

and handling of clients. For example, at most doctors' offices the front desk staff hollers out for "Mr. Smith, you can come on back" when it's a patient's turn to see the doctor. Many people take this as disrespect and resent it. They might not complain about it, but it leaves a sour taste and sabotages positive word of mouth. Teaching the staff to get up, come into the reception area and personally, politely, escort Mr. Smith back seems a little thing, yet it has big impact. A very successful Glazer-Kennedy member, Grant Miller, who owns a chain of tanning salons, substantially increased the value of each customer and overall sales by re-arranging the tanning beds and tour to begin with the best and priciest and end with the cheapest, the opposite of his industry norms. This is Sales Choreography®. Sydney's book is available at all booksellers or you can visit SydneyBarrows.com.

# CHAPTER 9

# The Postman as Your Salesman
## Using the Most Reliable Small-Business Marketing Media—Direct Mail

Dan Kennedy

Who still uses direct mail? Amazon.com. 1-800-Flowers. eBay. Yes, even companies you think of as e-commerce or online merchants mail hundreds of thousands or even millions of pieces of direct mail every year. Why? Because still, today, nothing drives sales like the mail.

*Do NOT listen to fools' pronouncements of the death or irrelevance of direct mail.* People running some of the most successful companies in the world, including those who are thoroughly committed to other media, do not neglect use of mail.

For the local small-business owner, direct mail serves a number of critical purposes no other media can.

## Permit Micro-Targeting

Nothing is more powerful in marketing than direct relevance of the marketer or merchant to the selected prospective customer, client, or patient. Nothing. And micro-targeted direct mail gives you the means of leveraging that. For example, for a group of financial advisors in the business of working with seniors and retirees, we are able to get, in their area, the names and addresses of not only married homeowners between the ages 57 and 71, but just those who contribute to charitable causes and who subscribe to financial and investment newsletters. But you will learn how to go even more micro with the information in this chapter, and the more micro, the more likely exceptionally good response is possible.

For a group of carpet-cleaning company owners I consulted with some years back, I taught them how to employ the classic five-house rule from the direct-sales business. That is, when you make a sale to Bob and Linda Jones, their immediate neighbors, one on either side and the three directly across the street, become "A+" prospects because they likely know and at least occasionally chat with Bob and Linda, and you can now reference Bob and Linda. The sales letter with piece of literature sent to each of those five homeowners specifically talks about what nice folks Bob and Linda are, and explains that it's your custom to offer "Good Neighbor New Customer" discounts and gifts to the immediate neighbors of customers. Since Bob and Linda just had their whole home's carpets made to look and feel like new, you, Ted and Carol, can too, and get a free dinner for two at a popular local restaurant as a gift just for inviting us out to do a Carpet Audit, and—well, you get the idea. The same principle can be used for just about any local business: restaurant, retail shop, hair salon, spa, insurance agency. And this strategy can create an endless chain of forced referrals. On average, with a three-step direct-mail campaign, entirely personalized as I just described, you can get at least one of the five to respond and become a customer, which immediately gives you five surrounding neighbors to mail to, which produces a customer, which immediately gives you five surrounding neighbors to mail to, ad infinitum. I call it *forced referrals* because often, the recipients of the mail will ask Bob and Linda about you and, presuming they're happy with you, Bob and Linda will give you a good recommendation when asked. If you simply asked Bob and Linda to take the initiative of telling their neighbors about you, they might, they might not, but they'll never tell your story as you can in a good sales letter, nor will they deliver the appealing offer you construct and present in your mailing.

Let me point out that no other media—other than knocking on doors in person, which tends to be unwelcome and inefficient—can give you this same micro-targeting, direct relevance, and forced referral opportunity (see Figures 9.1 and 9.2).

**FIGURE 9.1:** Five-House Plan

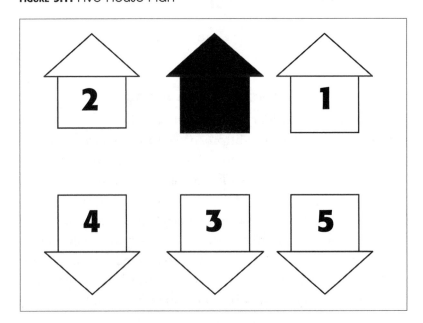

**FIGURE 9.2:** Five-House Multiplier

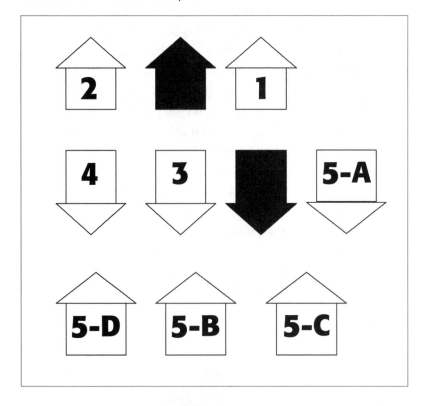

## Facilitate Precise Timing

As an example, consider birthdays. Dean Killingbeck at New CustomersNowMarketing (http://newcustomersnowmarketing. com or call 517-548-5522 ) provides restaurants and dozens of other kinds of businesses with mailings for and lists of people in an area around their business who are having birthdays this month. These prospective customers can then be sent a birthday-card style direct-mail piece with a sales letter and a coupon for a free dinner or other free gift. This acknowledges and utilizes the birthday. Other businesses, like spas, health clubs, cosmetic dentists, and financial advisors may time their mailings to the recipient's birthday month but not reveal they've done so. People are thinking more about dissatisfaction with their personal appearance, weight, or fitness or financial circumstances at birthday time than at most other times of the year. In this situation, a list of prospects surrounding the business gets divided into 12 lists based on birthday month. Either way, only direct mail can give you this kind of precision timing. (Even if you could get email addresses by birthday of "cold" prospects with whom you don't yet have a relationship, reaching out by email would be illegal spamming. If you could get phone numbers, you'd have the Do Not Call List law in your way. So far, there's no law against sending anybody a birthday card.)

## Reach Out to New Movers

This is timing related. People moving to a new area leave behind trusted doctors, accountants, family lawyers, favorite restaurants, tailors, dry cleaners, home repair providers, etc., and start out anew with no history and no loyalties. For this reason, they do get more direct mail right when they arrive at their new home, more than just about anybody else, so there is a lot of clutter, but most of it is, frankly, awful; it's rare that local merchants send them personalized, friendly, neighborly letters. Few display any persistence; most mail them once or twice and give up. This means you can win, and this is a game well worth winning. One of the grassroots strategies I teach to restaurants, retail shops, or groups of Main Street businesses going in together on welcome mailings is the promotion of the New Neighbor Event. It can be a designated night at the restaurant, a designated Saturday for the retailers. It can be restricted to those invited only or left open to all, but positioned as for new residents. That one time, held once a month, once every six weeks, or more often depending on the number of new residents, is positioned as a time and a place for new folks to congregate and meet each other. There's free food and drink, a free gift for everybody, prize drawings every hour, and any number of other incentives to participate.

If you really want to get grassrootsy, you'll go out and personally knock on the door, greet, and gift the new neighbor at their home. One of our Glazer-Kennedy Insider's Circle members who owns an upscale bakery in a relatively small community employs a person who does nothing but take fresh-baked pies and other desserts as welcome gifts to new residents' homes, getting to several each evening between 6:00 and 7:30 P.M.; no pitch, no coupons, just a welcome gift. A follow-up letter with a deadline-dated coupon is sent the next day. This same person takes fresh-baked breakfast pastries to new businesses in the area in the morning. The conversion rate on a series of mailings with various coupons and offers sent to the new neighbors personally welcomed and gifted in this manner is nearly 90%. If we consider the economics, this is a big win. A direct-mail sequence or multiple mailings over time to these new movers alone might pull as high as a 5% response rate. Thus, if that's three mailings times $1 each, it cost $300.00 to get 5 new customers, or $60.00 per customer. In this case, the employee, plus the pie or box of doughnuts, costs about $20 per delivery, so getting to 100 has $2,000.00 invested plus the investment in mailings of $300.00, for a total of $2,300.00. But if 70% of these 100 prospects come in and become customers, that's 70 customers acquired at a cost of $33.00 each—roughly half the net cost. And you buy speed: If you have 100 new move-ins a month to work with, one approach gets you only 5 new customers a month, the other gets 70. In 6 months' time, that's 30 versus 420; in a year, 60 vs. 840. Further, which customer do you think is more likely to bond with you and become a steady customer—the ones coming in just from coupons or the ones coming in ethically bribed with the extraordinary experience of having had a fresh-baked pie brought to their door by a friendly person welcoming them to their new home? And who is more likely to tell others about their experience?

Don't miss the point, though, that direct-mail follow-up makes this work. The gifting is done free of sales pitch or shoving coupons at the recipient. The mail permits multistep follow-up.

## Reach Out to Known Buyers

If you get someone to visit your website via advertising or search engine optimization or other means, you have a visitor with interest, but not a known buyer. If you exhibit at a local show or expo and collect contact information from people who stop at your booth, you have interested prospects, but not known buyers. By just about any means but direct mail to rented names of known buyers, you can't get known buyers! This is important because *a buyer is a buyer is a buyer*. So let's say you own a gourmet foods and wine shop. You could mail or otherwise advertise to everybody in your area and hope to reach and get the attention of people interested in and willing to pay premium prices for gourmet foods and fine wines. You could mail or otherwise advertise only to people in especially affluent neighborhoods near your shop, thus *improving the chances* of reaching and getting the attention of people interested in and willing to pay premium prices for gourmet foods and fine fines. Or you could rent the lists of *Wine Spectator* magazine and *Gourmet* magazine subscribers in your area—and stretch the size of that area because of their known interest—and mail to people you are virtually certain are spending money on gourmet foods and fine wines; at least we know they've spent money on subscriptions to the magazines. This process routinely used by all national direct-mail marketers is rejected by most small, local business owners because they find it too sophisticated or daunting, or because of the costs involved with renting buyer and subscriber names from commercial databases, but that's penny-wise and pound-foolish, as those costs are actually a good investment in efficiency. I have prepared a complete briefing on the use of such lists by small, local merchants, available free to readers of this book, available at www.NoBSBooks.com/grassroots.

## Switch B2B to Home Addresses

One of the problems with B2B marketing is Battleaxe Bertha, the gatekeeper, who blocks telephone prospecting like a good goalie on a hockey team, deletes email with abandon, and sorts and trashes inbound mail like a human paper shredder. Also, the small company owner, the dentist at his office, the retail store owner at his shop is busy and hurried during the day, and may harshly dispense with all attempts to reach him. But with most businesses and practices, at least 30% to 70% of the owners' home addresses can be obtained so mail can be sent to owners at their homes. I have a client who sells to dentists, who switched from advertising in the industry trade journals—which go to the office—mailing to and calling the offices, and sending email to the doctors, to mailing to those same doctors at their home addresses. He improved the total return on investment from his marketing efforts by 600%. These business owners' home address lists are relatively ordinary, so any good list broker should be able to assist you. However, if you need more assistance, check the Resources Directory for Glazer-Kennedy Insider's Circle members at the member site after accepting the free offer page 233.)

## Do Follow-Up

For many different kinds of businesses, I've developed what I call "Appointment, No Sale" direct-mail sequences, to follow up on prospects who come into showrooms, have face-to-face meetings with salespeople, get exams and recommendations from chiropractors, dentists, hearing aid specialists, etc., and don't immediately sign on the dotted line. You can see a sample and a complete explanation of this strategy at www.NoBSBooks.com/grassroots. But this is just one of a number of great applications for direct-mail follow-up. Another is for first-time customers: the simple, classic, personal, handwritten thank-you note, with a bounce-back gift card that has a redemption deadline. One of the most interesting tactics involves online to offline follow-up. A cosmetic dentist I've assisted with marketing for about 10 years has become very adept at driving local traffic to his website via various means, including the use of social media like Facebook, over 50 different YouTube videos, and search engine optimization. What he does that few others invest in doing, though, is getting full, physical contact information from those visitors by offering to send a free DVD and hardcover Smile Makeovers book, and then he does sequential, patient, persistent follow-up by direct mail. Before adding this, his conversion rate of website visitors to appointments within 90 days of visit to the site was below 2%. With this approach, it is nearly 15%. I also have a client who generates very large numbers of website visitors who asks only for their email address, but then has that email list appended to get their physical addresses, and sends the very same sales letter delivered to them online in printed form to all the nonbuyers, and converts an astounding 9% via that mailing!

The thing about follow-up in general is: Most businesspeople fail at it miserably. If you will discipline yourself and organize your business to capture full contact information from every prospect or new customer, and then diligently invest in persistent follow-up, you gain enormous competitive advantage. One of the most interesting examples of the power of follow-up, in a most unusual yet instructive business, is presented in my book *Making Them*

*Believe*, which I wrote with Chip Kessler, about one of the richest doctors at the turn of the century, judged a medical charlatan but nonetheless a national phenomenon. Dr. John Brinkley was the very first marketer of a cure for what we now politely call erectile dysfunction. His cure was to transplant goat glands—goats being known for randiness—to men's testicles. Yeccch, I know. But the doc is such an incredible case study in effective marketing we wrote an entire book about his exploits, and present a lesson in follow-up of high value to every business owner. If you would like information, visit www.ChipKessler.com, or obtain the book from any bookseller.

## Marry Direct Mail with All Other Grassroots Marketing

Every grassroots strategy, tactic, and method that Jeff or I present in this entire book can be aided before, during, or after its use by direct mail. For any sort of manual labor efforts such as telephone prospecting or telemarketing, dropping in at places of business, giving a speech at a local group's meeting, or exhibiting at a show or expo, direct mail can be used in advance to "soften the beachhead" and can be used afterward for follow-up.

As an example, the co-author of my *No B.S. Trust-Based Marketing* book, Matt Zagula, a very successful financial advisor, relies heavily on free-standing inserts in the newspaper to advertise his free workshops for seniors and retirees, and supports those with both TV and radio commercials in his area. But he also uses the newspaper sheet as a direct-mail piece to his list of accumulated, unconverted prospects to directly invite them to the next workshop. Also, everyone who attends but does not immediately book a private appointment gets a series of both direct-mail and email follow-up contacts. As another very grassrootsy example, one of my longest-time members, Dr. Nielsen, a chiropractor in a small town in Wisconsin, often turns a patient who has an interesting story and owns a local business into a "featured celebrity" in his newsletter, and then gets that article enlarged and framed to present to the patient, and most hang it in their office or other place of business. You now see doc's articles in a lot of different businesses in his community. Doc also uses these articles as direct-mail pieces (see Figure 9.3, page 140).

I saw a simple grassroots marketing effort occur in a small town I frequently visit, that could easily have been plus-ed with direct mail. The town has angle-parking on its main street, where shops and restaurants are, and on Friday evenings, quite a lot of people stroll about. This Friday there was also a music festival in the public park across from Main Street, so the crowd was multiplied. Parked in one of the spots was a minivan completely billboard-wrapped, advertising its owner's mobile auto-detailing business, and he had smartly stuck stacks of his own flyers under both his windshield wipers and business cards all along all the windows for people to take, turning his car into a gigantic "take-one box." I took a flier myself, and will soon call him to have my cars detailed at my home. He could have leveraged this by sending colorful postcards of his van to all the homes in the community or just those with owners of particularly nice cars, saying, "You probably saw my van parked on Main Street during Friday night's Music Festival, but you may not have picked up a flyer or jotted down my website or phone number—after all, you were there to enjoy the evening just as I was. That's why I've sent you this postcard, as a personal invitation to . . . " Just that reference, that reason-why for communicating, would likely bump his direct-mail response above what he would get without it. Then he could return to a street-level grassroots effort: Drive slowly through the neighborhoods he mailed into during dinner and early evening hours the week of his mailing, and during the Saturday of that week. He would get calls from people saying,

**FIGURE 9.3:** Doc's Direct Mail Piece

---

Waterford Doctor Swears Under Oath:

Copyright © 2001 - Dr. Nielsen

## "This Local Snowmobile Racer Does NOT Have Any Bionic Body Parts!"

Dear Friends:

The Waterford area has to be the best place on Earth. We have it all here: Skiing, snow, ice skating, snow, ice fishing, snow, freezing temps, snow boarding...and...SNOWMOBILING!

**The "Pepsi Kid" Rides A Rocket-Sled...With A Fuse!**

My good friend and long-time patient, Bill "Pepsi Kid" Buetow, is one of our many local sports celebrities. If you are familiar with Wisconsin snowmobile racing, you've definitely heard of him.

Recently, I watched Bill ride his "rocket-sled" before a race. I could be wrong, but I could swear that his sled is so powerful that he didn't turn a key to start it. He just lit a fuse...and hung on for the ride!

*Dr. Nielsen congratulates Bill Buetow (the "Pepsi Kid") after winning another grueling snowmobile race!*

**Precision Racing Machines Need Maintenance...And Riders Do Too**

Now, you can imagine what happens to a precision racing machine during a race. It hits bumps, it slides, it jerks all around, and it needs lots of special attention and maintenance.

It's really no different with snowmobile drivers and riders. They hit bumps, they get jerked around, and they get injured on occasion. And they also need periodic "precision tune-ups" and attention.

Bill doesn't have titanium arms, or legs...or...any other space-age body parts. And he periodically injures his neck and back while racing.

**The "Pepsi Kid" Is NOT Bionic**

And it's not uncommon to see him waiting at my front door (holding his neck or back) on Monday morning before we open.

Anyway, while I was treating Bill last Monday we started talking about doing a special promotion for other local residents who have headaches, neck pain, and back pain.

Bill told me that I could use him in my advertising ONLY if I ran a special promotion to raise money for the Waterford Fire and Rescue Squad. I agreed, and we're calling it...

**The Bionic Body Relief Program™**
(And It's Only Offered At My Office)

From now until March 31, 2001 anyone in the Waterford/Burlington area (who has never been to my office before...or anyone who hasn't been in for awhile) will receive their first visit FREE at my office.

However, there is a small catch. You have to make at least a $15 donation to the Waterford Fire and Rescue Squad.

**Now Offered For The First Time Ever...An "Iron-Clad" Satisfaction Guarantee!**

"The Bionic Body Relief Program™" is probably the finest program I've ever designed to treat your injuries. I want you to instantly realize how much your life can be improved with treatment at my office...therefore...your first office visit is GUARANTEED.

At the conclusion of your first visit, if you honestly think I've wasted your time, or you sincerely believe that you will not benefit from my care in any way...all you have to do is say so...and you will NOT have to make a $15 donation. In fact, I will make a donation to the Waterford Fire and Rescue in your name...if this happens!

The Bionic Body Relief Program™ Includes All Of The Following For A $15 Donation To The Waterford Fire & Rescue Squad:

□ *Private Health Consultation*
□ *Pain Pinpointing & Examination*
□ *Any Necessary X-Rays*
□ *A Four-Page Health Report*

**Why You Need This Program**

Ok, now imagine how life will be in a few weeks...if you do not handle your miserable injuries right now. How will your injuries effect your job? Will your injuries result in future arthritis? Will you be a fun person to be around at home? Or, work with? Ok, you get my drift...

**Call For Your FREE Visit Today**

It's easy to make an appointment. All you have to do is call my office right now at **(262) 534-3767** for *"The Bionic Body Relief Program™"*. We'll do everything possible to get you in the same day...even if we have to work you in during a busy time! We pride ourselves in being this area's "no waiting" office — *for busy people who need a "precision tune-up".* We're open 6 days a week and we're located near the Sentry Food Store, right behind the 76 Gas Station. And we accept most HMO patients!

**New Insurance & HMO Hotline (And Free Recorded Message)**

*Still not sure if your health insurance (or HMO) covers your care at my office?* It's easy to check your coverage. Just call us toll free: **1-800-359-3765 Ext. #4** (24 Hrs). All you have to do is leave your name, phone number, and the name of your insurance plan. We'll check it out and call you back as soon as possible!

**Waterford Chiropractic Office**
Dr. G.E. Nielsen * docnielsen@aol.com
**505 Aber Drive, P.O. Box 86
Waterford, WI 53185-0086**

"Hey, I saw your van on Main Street, I got your postcard, and I saw you in my neighborhood the other night while I was watering the lawn . . ."

---

## Use Direct Mail to Nurture and Maintain Relationships with Customers

There's probably no company more sophisticated at use of online media than Disney. They have essentially unlimited resources, extremely talented and creative people at their disposal, vaults of video and pictorial content, and they do have millions of customers engaged online, in different fan clubs, activity sites, online vacation planning, and more. As Disney Vacation Club Members, Carla and I have access to online resources exclusively for us. And as D23 fan club members, we have access to exclusive new videos every week, archives, an online store, and more. Yet, Disney very frequently sends us direct-mail packages, selling additional Vacation Club points, the newest Club resorts and destinations, asking for referrals, promoting D23 events and more, plus a monthly *Vacation Club* magazine and a quarterly *D23* magazine in the mail. Why? Because there's probably no company smarter about nurturing and maintaining a strong bond and relationship with customers for life than Disney, and they know there's just no substitute for the experience of receiving, opening, and having attention captured by good direct mail.

## The Two Biggest Advantages You CAN Get with Direct Mail

*First, you can show up as no one else does.* Most other media is limited in format "Imagineering"—to borrow a Disney word—and there's a lot of me-too-ishness to it. But bound only by the value of the obtained customer, direct-mail offers unlimited opportunity for dramatic and unusual presentation. Mail can be delivered in odd envelopes, tubes, boxes, lunch bags. Objects with short messages on them can be mailed as is; I have clients who have mailed basketballs, coconuts, and canoe paddles. "Object enclosed" mail—sometimes called "lumpy mail"—

utilizing all sorts of *freemiums* and ad specialty items, creates curiosity because the lumpiness, or rattle in the box, or label (such as, "Handle with Care. TOY SURPRISE INSIDE") creates physical engagement, and can obligate the recipient to giving your message consideration. Humor can even be utilized, as with the mailings sent with coffee-cup-sized plastic or aluminum trash cans and a note saying, "You've thrown my two previous letters in the trash, so I sent you a trash can. I'd rather you kept it to keep paper clips or candy in, but if you must, you can use it to throw this last letter out in. However: I do have something quite important to tell you about . . ."

In different campaigns for different purposes, here are some of the things I've delivered with sales letters:

1. Oven mitts
2. Baseball cards
3. Boxes of animal crackers
4. Toy dump trucks
5. Packages of Bayer Aspirin
6. Small plastic magnifying glasses
7. Clocks
8. Stuffed animals
9. Shoes
10. Giant erasers labeled, "For Big Mistakes"
11. Chocolate chip cookies
12. Luggage tags

Some of the themes you can use are:

1. Caution: The information enclosed is too hot to handle!
2. It's time to dump all the old ideas about . . .
3. If your current XYZ supplier is giving you headaches . . .
4. As you can see, I've enclosed a magnifying glass to help you more clearly see . . .
5. Time's running out!

My friends at 3-D Mail Results are the reigning experts in sourcing and matching items like this with different themes for direct-mail campaigns, and I suggest checking them out at www.3dmailresults.com.

*The second related advantage you can give yourself with direct mail is: being paid attention to rather than being ignored.* When you select and single out a small enough number of high-value, high-probability prospects, and show up like no one else via packages like I've just described, you make it almost impossible for your prospective customer or client to ignore you or, in B2B settings, for a gatekeeper to easily discard your missive. You can also essentially ethically bribe the recipient into giving your message more time and consideration than he otherwise would when the package he receives is especially clever and/or contains a gift of some kind he likes and keeps. Jeff and his brother Marc did a very successful lumpy campaign by mailing out a number of autographed copies of one of his *Street Fighter* books to the CEOs and CMOs of medium and large franchise companies. That very targeted mailing led to a couple of big consulting contracts.

With leads generated by your own advertising or by grassroots activities, you can use this approach to blow competitors out of the water. For example, if you call most home improvement companies and ask for a brochure, if you get anything, it'll be a brochure, unless you happen to call one of the home improvement companies I've advised. If you go to a home improvement business's website, you'll likely see whatever you see there, then possibly get follow-up emails—unless you happen to call one of the home improvement companies I've advised. In that case, you'll get what I call a "shock 'n' awe package," with a collection of literature; a 12-page illustrated sales letter; an infomercial-style DVD with actual customers showing off the work done in their homes and giving testimonials; a tin of popcorn and two carefully-wrapped bottles of old-fashioned root beer to enjoy while you watch the DVD, a Personal Planning Guide with checklists for every imaginable home improvement project, and a 5-Point Peace-of-Mind Guarantee certificate personalized to the prospect and hand-signed by the company owners. Since most people contact more than one home improvement company at the same time, who do you think wins the battle for guaranteed attention to a lengthy, thorough presentation?

## The Ultimate Grassroots Direct-Mail Marriage Strategy

I'll close with a story that reveals a very powerful strategy:

One day, in the mail, I got a hand-addressed envelope, addressed to me, bearing a first-class stamp, from a business peer; not really a friend, more of an acquaintance. We were in the same kind of business, belonged to the same association, and happened to live in the same city. Since I recognized his name in the return address, and he had personally sent it to me, it passed the trash-sort test, went in my "A-pile," and shortly, I personally opened it and read it. I was curious.

Let me stop there for just a moment. With direct mail, three things must happen for you to have opportunity. Your piece must get delivered, get opened, and get read. None of those things can be taken for granted. All three have to happen. Similarly, a radio commercial must be aired during a program your best prospects listen to, must be heard, and make them jot down a phone number or website, if not instantly call. A lot of people mentally tune out commercials. Email must get delivered, opened and read, too, and any pro at email marketing will tell you that deliverability, open rate, and readership are all problematic. So the fact that this tactic I've described here got me to take this letter, sit down in my chair absent any distractions, open it, and read it with curiosity is very significant.

The letter began: "Hi. I guess we haven't talked or caught up in a while. And this may seem odd, but I'm writing to you about my plumber." His letter went on to tell me about a pipe at his home springing a leak right before a party—to which I was not invited by the way—and his heroic and reliable plumber responding immediately and saving the day. The letter cautioned me that most homes five years old or older have such disasters waiting to occur without warning at the worst possible time, and the water damage can not only be disruptive but expensive. His plumber, however, would come out and give my home the most thorough inspection ever, so no tragedy like this would ever happen to me. And, whether I took him up on that offer or not, I should keep Al the Plumber's info handy for the day I needed the most expert, most honest, most reliable, most heroic plumber who ever lived: a guy so impressive that he, my business acquaintance, was moved to write to people he knew, endorsing the guy. The term for this is an "endorsed mailing." It is engineered with a willing, extremely satisfied customer or client who has some influence with a list of good prospects. Often your customers are happy to do it if nicely asked and the letter is written for them and the work is done for them as well. The response to such a mailing, provided it includes an offer anybody can immediately respond to, can be very good. The lists are usually small but mighty, so the cash outlay is small, and the return on investment very high.

I'd love to tell you the rest of the Al the Plumber story, because I did call him, did get that inspection, and did spend some money with him, preventing tragedy, and did enroll in his VIP Club, for maintenance and guaranteed emergency response. But this chapter is already over-long. Suffice it to say, Al did just fine with this endorsed mailing if I was the only customer gained. And by quizzing him, I know I wasn't.

This is grassroots, because it requires you to personally take your client out to lunch or sit down with him and ask for this favor and describe how it works, secure permission, draft the letter to come from him, get some of his stationery, or have some made for him, get envelopes hand-addressed, and stamps licked. Each endorsed mailing requires this personal effort. Each letter from each endorser will be a bit different. It can, however, be an extremely productive way to leverage your customer with a significant circle of influence.

To close the subject of direct mail, as far as it can be taken within this book, I would insist that no grassroots marketing program is really complete without including smart uses of direct mail. The postman is still the only salesman who works for the price of a stamp or a few stamps, carries your letter or package to the door, and if need be, rings twice.

## Learn More. Get Very Smart. Profit from Direct Mail. Yes, You Can.

Hopefully this chapter motivates you to get serious about using direct mail successfully for your business. There is a learning curve requiring more information than can be provided in a single chapter. This is my number-one area of specialization as a consultant and copywriter, so I've written extensively about it. You'll get a much more complete understanding from my books *The Ultimate Sales Letter* and *No B.S. Direct Marketing for Non-Direct Marketing Businesses*, available at all booksellers. Further, you'll discover a whole world of marketing opportunities for your business notably including effective use of direct mail by accepting the FREE OFFER provided on page 233.

# CHAPTER 10

# Fools Rush In

## How to Use—and How to Waste Dollars on—the Internet and Other Technology Media

Jeff Slutsky

The internet can be an effective marketing tool for a local "brick and mortar" business. But since the internet, including your website, is just one of many different tools at your disposal, you want to ensure that a disproportionate amount of your resources are not tied up into one, ever-changing marketing tool.

### Your Website

For most local businesses, the web can be a great additional tool, but it's just that . . . additional. Unless you have a full-blown e-commerce function and plan to do business all over the world, you need to focus your efforts on the web at a level that makes sense for you.

First of all, you should have a website. Many potential customers will want to look at your site before they call or visit you in person. In that regard, your site is more a "disqualifier" than anything else. That is, they'll look at your site to make sure you can solve their problem.

Therefore, you need a presence on the web, but one that is just good enough to do the job. It is possible to spend a small fortune on your website. For most small, local businesses, a huge expense developing your site can't be justified based on the potential return. There are likely much more effective ways to spend your limited marketing dollars. So when planning your website, plan for something very simple that does the job and doesn't cost a lot of money.

Your web developer can probably use an existing template that allows you to plug in your elements. Make sure it's clean, easy to read, and provides the information you think your customers need to feel comfortable contacting you by email, phone, fax, or visit. Think of your website as an interactive brochure about your business. One of the biggest mistakes you can make is to let some technical parasite convince you to buy a much more elaborate site that you need. Here are some key issues to keep in mind regarding your site:

1. As you are designing it, be sure to incorporate all the optimization tactics mentioned earlier.
2. You should be able to easily update information yourself. You shouldn't have to pay someone every time you want to make a simple copy change, add content, or add a photograph.
3. Make sure your homepage loads quickly. Many sites feature bells and whistles to make them more interesting, like Flash. The problem with Flash is that it takes a long time to load and most people don't have the patience. If you're going to use Flash, video, or anything that takes time to load, it should be on deeper pages in your site. Flash is

also not visible to Apple product users, so avoid it if you are concerned with the type of customers who will use local search to find you with their iPhone or iPad.

4. Provide a printable version of your information. Make it easy for a prospective buyer to print out your information so it is easily read and used.

5. On every page, no matter where they are in your site, always have contact information so visitors can call, email, or fax you. Don't make them look for "Contact us" to find out how to get in touch with you.

6. Test your email addresses connected to your site. Make sure that everything works right, because if someone is sending you an email and for some reason it's not getting to you, you may never know about it. It could be a lost opportunity. I suggest that you send yourself an email at least once a week to test your connections.

7. Decide how often you need to add or change things. Is it important for your site to bring the same person back repeatedly? Or is its purpose for a potential first-time buyer to feel comfortable enough with you to actually pay you a visit at your location? There's a big difference between the two objectives, and each requires very different tactics, so think it through carefully. If you feel it is important to bring people back to the site often, you're going to be spending a lot of time coming up with new content and a reason for them to visit you.

8. Even if you don't have a lot of capability to make changes yourself, you might want to at least set up a few special pages that allow you to personally upload your information. This could be as simple as weekly specials that show photos and simple copy.

Now that you have a website, you need to get people to go to it. Just because you have one doesn't mean you'll get traffic on it automatically. For a local business with limited marketing dollars available, you want to be very stingy about how you market your site. You have to make the decision whether to spend your marketing dollars to get people to your site, or to your business.

## Search Engine Optimization

Natural search engine optimization (SEO) of your website allows you to get more potential buyers to find your site when they are using a search engine. When a potential buyer conducts a search via a search engine (i.e., Yahoo!, Google, MSN, etc.), they'll enter some "keywords" or "key phrases." Your success in getting people to your website is directly related to your position on the results page when the search is conducted. According to 10X Marketing, a private research firm, "Those businesses that appear on the first page of these searches are getting 50% to 70% of the business from these customers." For a company that depends on their website for a major portion of their business, the difference between appearing on page one or page two can literally mean tens of thousands of dollars a day in lost sales. Car rental companies and other travel-related businesses, for example, know that the higher up they appear on the page, the more money they make.

To make sure these types of companies stay high up on the results listings, they turn to specialists that may cost thousands of dollars a month. For larger companies who rely heavily on their website for purchases or reservations, it's well worth it. As a local company you might be hard pressed to see a return on your investment, since you use your website as a supplement to your overall marketing efforts. Jason Harris of CeraNet, Inc., (www.cera.net) is one of those specialists who suggests several simple modifications you can make to your site to get it to list higher during a search.

For the biggest return for the least amount of effort and cost, Jason suggests the optimization effort be focused on: the title bar, content, meta tags, press releases, submissions, and links.

To see how this works, Jason had us select three keywords or phrases that we felt people might use in trying to find us or our subject matter. The three we chose were:

1. Jeff Slutsky
2. Neighborhood marketing
3. Guerrilla marketing

Consider someone wanting to find a company that could help them with their neighborhood marketing. They would go on Google or Yahoo! and in the search box type, "neighborhood marketing." When Jason showed us this, *Street Fighter Marketing* only shows up at the fifth listing, but that listing is for an article we wrote for *Pizza Marketing Quarterly* magazine, and the link goes to their site, not ours. For the best results, you want to appear as high up as possible on the page after a search. Better yet, it would be great if your listings are in the first five that show up. This would help bypass many of your competitors.

Given the weak response to our "neighborhood marketing" search, Jason made several recommendations of inexpensive changes to our website to move us up in the rankings.

### *Content*

The next resource that the search engines look for, according to Jason, is content. The more the better. One other key phrase that we wanted to use was "guerrilla marketing." Many people use this as a generic term for local or neighborhood marketing. Jay Conrad Levinson did a brilliant job of branding the "guerrilla" series. Though we actually do entirely different types of work, from a search engine standpoint, many people looking for our type of service will use "guerrilla" in their search.

With a "guerrilla marketing" key phrase search, our Grassroots Marketing site did not make the list for at least the first 12 pages. Since 70% of the action is on the first page, our goal was to get a listing as close to the first page as possible. To do this we needed to use the phrase "guerrilla marketing" in the content of our site.

Additionally, we added several pages of content about that subject. For six years we had written a weekly column for the Knight Ridder/Tribune News Service, so we have a collection of over 500 different articles. Several of them were about co-authors of Levinson's who wrote books in the Guerrilla series. These included *Guerrilla Tele-Selling*, *Guerrilla PR*, and *Guerrilla Negotiations*. So these articles were added to the other articles on our website. Jason also suggested that we do a quick rewrite and add "guerrilla marketing" two to three times per page, as long as it made sense in the article. In this way the search engines were more likely to snag our site when a search was conducted.

Jason also warned that we shouldn't overdo it. You don't want to be accused of "keyword stuffing" or "keyword spamming." Some people try to get more responses by mentioning a keyword 20 or more times in an article. This is not advised as it is possible for the search engines to blacklist you if you practice that extreme approach.

### *Meta Tags*

Meta tags are pieces of information placed in a web page not intended for users to see, but which typically pass information to search engine crawlers, browser software, and some other applications. The most common meta tags relevant to search engines are keyword and description tags. Unlike normal HTML tags, meta tags do not affect how the page is displayed. Many search engines use this information when building their indices.

Meta tags are useful in providing your site with variations of keywords. There are a number of ways people might try to spell "Slutsky." To make it easy for the search engines to find your site, include every misspelled version of your keywords that you can use. For ideas, look at your junk mail.

Those pieces are probably a good indication as to the more common misspellings. For "Slutsky" we've seen: slutzky, slutski, slutzski, flutsky, slusky, lutsky, stutsky, and the worst one—shitsky. These are now appearing as meta tags on our website. We do the same with "guerrilla": gorilla, gorila, gurilla, guerrila, guerila, guerilla, etc.

To begin the optimizing process for your website, your first step is to write down all the keywords and phrases that you think potential customers might use who are in the market for your products or services. Start with the obvious. When we searched "Jeff Slutsky," our website was the very first listing. This is good news. However, when we search "Slutsky," which could be the way many do search for us, it's a different story. You would think that "Slutsky" would not be that common of a name. In my Google search for "Slutsky" I discovered that *Slutsky* is the 78,019th *most* popular *last* name in the *United States*. According to the 1990 United States Census (http://www.census.gov), the name's frequency is 0.000%; percentile is 89.455. But as uncommon as it is, there are several other Slutskys getting more cyber attention than I. The list topper is Eugene (Yevgeni) Slutsky (1880–1948), a Russian economist who created something called the Slutsky Theorem. As far as we know, we're not related. But we do know that he has nothing to do with marketing. The famous Slutsky equation is: $(\partial X/\partial pi)$ $y = (\partial X/\partial pi)u - xi(\partial X/\partial y)P$. I have no idea what this means other than Eugene dominates the result pages. If it wasn't for QuickBooks I couldn't even balance my checkbook. There's also a famous Russian poet named Boris Slutsky, a dentist in Philadelphia, a poster artist named Stan, and an intellectual property lawyer in Atlanta. There are a few listings referencing us from speaker bureaus, but it's not until the second to the last listing on the ninth page does a link to our website show up. Thus, the challenge remains, how does "Jeff Slutsky" and in particular, "Jeff Slutsky" on the Grassroots Marketing website, start to show up higher in a search for "Slutsky"? (Thank goodness my last name wasn't Smith.)

After you've created this list of keywords and phrases, prioritize them. For our exercise, we chose three; however, that list could be many more. Each individual word and phrase will need its own list of actionable steps to optimize your results. Try to determine which ones are most likely to be used by your potential buyers to find a website that will help with your product or service. Go on Yahoo!, Google, and MSN and search each of the words or phrases to see where you appear, if at all, in the results from the search.

Once you see where you are on the list, your effort will go into moving your website up that list. Take the first keyword or phrase on your list and do the same three things that Jason did for us. First, add it to the title bar on your home page and all other relevant pages in your site. Next, create some content about that subject. This can be an article. Use that keyword or phrase three times on each web page of that article. If your article is long, you can break it up into a number of different pages. (Each page should be around 500 words.) Two pages with 500 words are better than one page of 1,000 words from a search engine perspective. Third, add that keyword or phrase into your meta tags, including all the misspelled or misused versions of it that you're aware of. Is there a word or phrase that customers use where they might have you confused with another site? Then go back and follow the same process for the second word or phrase on your list.

The first keyword on your list should be your company name. If someone is already aware of your business and they simply want additional information or a way to contact you, don't make it difficult for them to track you down. This is the low-hanging fruit, so pick it first. Then start to work your key product or services lines.

### Press Releases

Sending out press releases through the right sources can dramatically move you up in the search. Sending out your release through a service like PR Newswire (www.prnewswire.com) will get it looked at by numerous sites. Your release should be keyword focused. You may not get any response to do articles about you in the media, but even so, sending out these releases will help drive your site higher up in order. Using the same keyword focus, you can run a campaign every month for four or five months. According the Jason, Tuesday and Wednesday are the best days for sending out these releases.

### Submissions

Submission to the search engines and directories is very important to do at least once. Some people like to resubmit every so often, but that first submission is critical to getting the engines aware of your existence. There is some legwork involved, in that you have to go to each engine's site and find the form, fill it out, and submit it.

### Links

One other way search engines evaluate your site's relevance is the number of other sites that point to yours. If a given site scores really high and also points to your site, there's a good chance it will help improve your site's visibility. When possible, you might want to get reciprocal links to and from your site.

### Sponsored Links: Pay Per Click

Google, Yahoo!, and others provide an advertising service where interested surfers can go from their site to your site with a click. They charge you for each click. It sounds like a no-lose proposition, but if you're not careful, you could end up paying hundreds of dollars a month for this service. That would be fine, of course, if the cost generated a reasonable amount of new sales for you.

Don R. has a marketing company that specializes in printing posters. He gets a fair amount of his business through his website. Using AdWords and others, he increased the traffic and sales on his website. The problem was the increase in sales did not cover the advertising cost. As in any type of marketing, you must use it wisely to make it worth your while.

We tried this on our own site. By googling "Jeff Slutsky" we saw that there were a number of sponsored links popping up

## Attack Plan

The key phrase "motivational speaker" is a problem for us. We don't consider ourselves "motivational" speakers as such, since we provide a lot of content in our talks, but that might be the phrase people use to research possible keynote speakers. To increase the likelihood of getting noticed by the search engines, we:

1. Put the phrase "motivational speaker" in several of the title bars;

2. Added a couple of articles about "motivational speakers" on our site, the key phrase mentioned three times in each page;

3. Where it made sense, added the key phrase to other parts of our site in our descriptions;

4. Arranged reciprocal links to other motivational speakers, especially those with a great deal of web visibility;

5. Added "motivational speaker" to the meta tags, including other variations like "motivational speaking" and "inspirational speaker."

Once you get someone to your site, your goal is to get that person to take some kind of action. With that in mind, you'll want to modify your website accordingly.

from speaker bureaus. They were paying money to have access to people looking for me. It's great to have speaker bureaus aggressively marketing me, but if someone is looking specifically for me instead of a speaker on marketing, one of those choices should be us! So, we started paying per click so that if someone searches specifically for "Jeff Slutsky" we would be one of the first choices. We started to get charged a couple hundred dollars a month and weren't getting any actual bookings from it. We clearly didn't know what we were doing, so we dropped it.

## Web Coupons: Be Careful

With the success of Groupon, Living Social, and a number of others, businesses have an emerging opportunity to promote trial and get new customers. The way most of them work is that you offer to provide your product or service for at least half off. The web coupon company will use their website and email list to sell gift certificates to your business, and they'll split the sales with you, so, you'll end up getting 25% (or less if you offer a greater discount) on those sales. Many small businesses complain that they couldn't make any money with these services because of the deep discount, or they've been overwhelmed by demand from those who purchased them. I say they just didn't know how to use them right.

### *What's Your Objective?*

If you're going to use one of these coupon services you have to understand what you want out of it. Don't plan on making any money on these transactions. In fact, it's possible to lose a little on each one. The purpose of this is to introduce your business to a lot of potential new customers with no upfront advertising cost. Think about it. You only end up paying if there is a buying customer coming into your front door. Then it's up to you to make sure they want to come back.

Offer a price that makes sense for you. You could offer ten dollars' worth of services for five. Or you could offer $20 worth of services for $10. Which makes the most sense for you? You would be better off making an offer that requires the new customer to pay a little bit more out of pocket. So if your average sale is around $12, then $10 for $5 should get you at least $2 more of regular sales. You'll have made $2.50 from Groupon plus another $2 from the add-on sale.

The other option you have is to limit the number of units coupon services can sell. If you can't handle more than 500 over a six-month period, arrange it so the online offer stops after they've sold 500.

### *Don't Be So Quick to Repeat Your Success*

If your online promotion is a great success, don't do it again for at least another year. You've already introduced your business to that audience. Offering another big discount to the same group just doesn't make sense—unless you do something completely different. One of our restaurant chain clients first did a $12 for $6 offer, and then came back a couple of months later to promote catering with a $100 for $50 offer. Catering is an entirely different animal, so it made sense to have a specific offer just for that.

## Getting More Visitors to Your Site

There are two main ways that potential buyers can find your website when they're searching for you using the main search engines or browser. The link to your site will show either through a *sponsored link* or through the *standard link*. A sponsored link, as the name implies, requires that you pay a fee to get the listing when a keyword is being searched. That fee is generally a PPC (pay-per-click). The standard links are a little more complicated. The way you appear on a page or even if you appear on a page of search results depends on a number of different factors relating to your website. The modifications made to a website to get higher on that list of search results are called "optimization."

## Start Marketing Your Website with Free Exposure

Put your website address or URL on all the marketing and advertising pieces that you are using already. Anyplace you would put your phone number, also include your web address. This costs you nothing. This includes your business cards, letterhead, and any media advertising, on the side of your trucks and so on.

Beyond that, it depends what type of business you have to determine whether it makes sense to pay money to drive traffic to your site. Remember, if you're using your site as a supplement to your other marketing, it may not make sense to seek business on a national level by marketing your website directly. However, if you run a specialty business, or you're able to offer a unique value or service that people might not be able to obtain locally, then it may make sense.

### *Monetizing Your Site*

Jason recommended that we consider adding some links from our site to other sites that would pay us a commission for items sold. He called this "monetizing" our site. We were concerned that it might cheapen our site and we'd lose integrity; however, if those links made sense in some way, it could be a big advantage to our readers.

For your website, determine if there are possible links that provide your readers added value and at the same give you the potential of earning a little extra money. You want to make sure that any other URLs you refer make sense based on the type of product or service you provide. Also, does your URL attract the wrong group because the name may be confusing? If so, find out which sites they really wanted and see if you can work out an associate relationship with them.

## Constantly Changing

The digital world is changing daily so it's critical that you keep up with new development. Though the ideas suggested in this chapter have been successful strategies, it's very likely that there are new ideas and different approaches now that were not available when we wrote this manuscript. Regardless, digital and social media are a big part of the marketing landscape. Be careful not to spend tons of marketing dollars on it before you know what will work and what will not. As a small-business owner, it doesn't often pay to be the pioneer. Let someone else do the experiment. Be aware of it, and when the time is right, start gradually adding digital marketing to your marketing mix.

# CHAPTER 11

# The Magical Mystery Bus
## Old and New Marketing Media Traveling Together

Jeff Slutsky

O utdoor advertising is perhaps one of the oldest forms of advertising. It can be very costly, so with all the different options, other media, road distractions, and competition for drivers, you want to look at unique ways of maximizing this resource.

## Vehicle Advertising

You can get free advertising exposure with your vehicles. Being clever with it will get you even more attention. Driving around town can be one of your best forms of advertising, according to Jeff Whiting of Help! Wizards, a Columbus, Ohio, computer consulting firm that makes house calls. In October of 1999, they bought their first vehicle. Instead of going with a white van as they originally thought, they decided to buy something that would attract more attention. So they bought a bright yellow Volkswagen Beetle. Their "Help! Wizards" logo is boldly blazoned on both sides of the bug and their trademark "!" is on the hood. They've since added three more Bugs to the fleet and have two more scheduled to hit the streets very soon. And the results? According to Whiting, they get at least one call a week directly from the exposure to the "Wizard Bug."

And speaking of bugs, an independent extermination company in Fort Wayne, Indiana, used an old hearse with a big bug on top as its vehicle. It got a lot of attention, but many customers felt uncomfortable with that in their driveways.

If you would prefer to make your point more subtly, consider getting promotional vanity tags for your car. The right message can generate some interest. The plates that seem to make the most impact are the ones that take a few moments for you to figure out. They engage you, and then once you finally "decode" the plate's meaning, you remember it forever. Here are some other tags that we've seen or have been submitted to us:

- "MR 2TH" we assume is a dentist.
- "I SUE 4 U" from a lawyer in California.
- "1099" or "W 2" is what we suggested to our CPA brother, Howard Slutsky.
- "401K" for an investment advisor specializing in retirement accounts.
- "BUYLOW" for a stockbroker.
- "P8NTR" we guess is a painter.
- "MNIPUL8" and "SPINE" are from chiropractors.
- "EIEIO" suggested a farm co-op manager.
- "U P 4 ME" is from an urologist in New Orleans.

One of the members of the audience of a keynote speech we were giving told us about the man who had one delivery vehicle. A friend of his who had a large fleet made fun of his single truck. So he had some magnetic signs made with his company logo on it. He also put at the bottom under the logo "Delivery Vehicle #1," which went on the left side. "Delivery Vehicle #2" was placed on the right side of the truck. On the back was "Delivery Vehicle #3." His friend was amazed at how fast his fleet grew.

When considering signage for your vehicles, don't forget to include all sides—left, right, and back. If you do create a moving billboard with your vehicles, it must be very clear to your drivers that they have to be courteous drivers, no matter what. Even a justifiable flipping off of a road-rage ravaged, cell phone-talking lane hog can create a great deal of negative ill-will and bad word-of-mouth.

For temporary vehicle signs, consider the use of vehicle magnets. They can be very big impact in full color if you want. This would be a great way to promote something that you do not want to be on your vehicles permanently. You can even run monthly or seasonal specials using this approach. For example, a heating and cooling company could produce magnetic signs that promote preseason maintenance of your furnace or air conditioner. The signs are used during the slower time leading up to the busy season when the weather changes.

If your company is sponsoring a local sports team or league, in addition to the normal exposure you get on the jerseys and signage at the playing field, make part of the deal that all the parents have to use your window decal in the back of their car. Parents usually have bumper stickers or window decals of the sport anyway, only you provide them some which include the wording, "Sponsored by (your company)." In this way your dozens, if not hundreds, of cars provide you additional exposure at no additional cost. This extends your exposure beyond the group itself and may be the tipping point for justifying your sponsorship in respect to ROI.

Graphics for vehicles can be very dramatic, thanks to digital printing capabilities. Your vehicles are moving billboards, and except for the cost of creation and application, your message is distributed free. Of course, if you're going to use your vehicles in this way, make sure they are always clean. And when not in use, park them, if possible, in a high-traffic area so they still provide you additional free exposure.

## Yard Signs

While researching the home improvement industry for a keynote speech to the National Association of Remodeling Industry (NARI), I discovered a piece of research that showed that 75% of remodeling jobs were generated by the yard sign used by the remodeling company at the job site. All other forms of marketing, combined, didn't even come close. These inexpensive, and in many cases, disposable signs have the power to grab the attention of potential buyers. One reason seems to be that the sign shows that the company is doing the work for a neighbor. It's a form of referral and integrity. If that same sign was planted at a busy corner, it might not have the same impact even though the traffic count was significantly higher. While consulting with Curb Light Appeal, a residential landscape lighting and design company, I told the owner, Eddy, about those stats. So he ordered yard signs for his business. Sure enough, they generated qualified leads.

Getting permission from the customer is key when using this type of sign. One way to work it in is if the customer is asking for some kind of price consideration which you are willing to do anyway to get the job, make part of the deal that they must let you display your yard sign during the job and 14 to 30 days following it. You can even bump your prices a little in anticipation of that.

When you quote the job, you can say the regular price is X, "But if you let us display our yard sign for 30 days, we'll knock $500 off the price."

Since yard signs are very small, it's important to make your message painfully simple. One element says what is being done. Another element is the phone number. It could be something like the one in Figure 11.1.

Pay the extra money to have the signs printed on both sides. Use simple, easy-to-read type and high-contrast colors between the background and the lettering. When placing the sign, make sure it's in a spot that is easy to read from passing traffic. For a corner home, you want two signs for each direction.

Yard signs only work for those types of services that "improve" the home. You would not likely get permission if you market bug extermination, leaky basement repair, toxic waste

**FIGURE 11.1:** Yard Sign

removal, or anything that requires a level-three HazMat suit or forces your house to be sealed in plastic like at the end of E.T.

## Billboards

The granddaddy of outdoor advertising is the billboard. Billboards make impact, no doubt. It can be a very creative medium. The only question is whether you can buy your billboards so that you get a good return. Billboards can be expensive. If you have a location that hasn't high visibility, a billboard can help direct traffic to you. But to bring in paying customers, is your money better spent elsewhere? The only way to know for sure is trying and tracking. Sometimes the price of the boards is negotiable and sometimes not. Plus you have to consider the cost of production as well. Currently the standard is to produce your message on vinyl, which could cost you as much as a month or more of the board itself.

---

## NO B.S. GRASSROOTS MARKETING INCONVENIENT TRUTH #9

Billboards are only useful if drivers can read them. Limit the copy to no more than three elements, six words, clean type, and a simple, easy-to-understand message.
If you can't do that, don't waste your money.

---

Location is important as well. Usually the billboard companies price their boards on what they call a gross rating point or GRP showing. This term has no relation to the GRPs used in broadcast advertising. One rating point equals 1% of the market's population. What you want to find out is the *annual ADT* (annual average daily traffic). This is the total number of vehicles passing the location in 24 hours based on counts taken over an entire year. Like in broadcast, you can figure out your CPM (cost per thousand) based on the relationship of the ADT to the price.

Also, consider doing a *pre-ride*. Drive by each location you're considering to evaluate the *approach*. This is the distance measured along the line of travel from the point where the billboard first becomes fully visible to the point where the copy is no longer readable. See if there are any obstructions that may cut down on the visibility of your board. If it's winter, anticipate leaves on a nearby tree in spring. If it's summer, anticipate earlier sundown on the drive home from work. Are those boards lighted, and if so, at what time are the lights set to come on? Drive the locations during rush hour in each direction. See how much time people are spending at that location. Are they driving into the sun and therefore not seeing your board? Is traffic flow unencumbered so there is less time to look at billboards? What else is at that location that is competing for the driver's attention? It could be other boards, signage, displays, scenery, etc. As long as you're going to make a sizable investment, it's best to know exactly what you're getting for your money.

If you can't get the billboard company to come down on the price, see if they have some not-so-desirable locations that they're having trouble selling (usually in nonelection years). To create additional exposure, ask for some bonus boards, but you want them after your main campaign is running so you can use the existing vinyl instead of paying for extra. What do they do with the vinyl after the campaign is over? It could make a very interesting backdrop for a trade show booth, or perhaps it could be installed on the side of your building, if permitted.

More elaborate versions of billboards are *wallscapes* and *spectaculars*. Wallscapes are advertisements painted directly on building walls. Some walls can accommodate vinyl facings that are secured in a frame. Both have large-scale exposure and high visibility to vehicular and pedestrian traffic. They are generally geared for high-density areas like downtowns.

Spectaculars are usually larger than 14' x 48' and positioned at prime locations in a market. Both require custom designing and are intended for long-term exposure. Obviously they are very costly so you have to evaluate very carefully what your objectives are in choosing this type of outdoor medium.

## Inflatables and Costumes

If you have a reasonably high visibility location, inflatable displays and mascot costumes can really draw extra attention to your business at a very low cost. The Firestone Mastercare down the street from our office has a three-story-high inflatable tire that they display three or four times a year. It's obviously shared with their other locations and rotates from store to store. You can't help but see it. The only negative for this tire display is they have to make sure it's always inflated. When you're trying to convey the quality of your tires, a huge tire that is going flat and flapping in the wind will not help your cause.

During tax season, the Liberty Tax mascot was out by the street waving at cars. Their office was in a strip center with no visibility from a very busy street. The mascot drew attention to the location at a very little cost. And your cost of that costume is tax deductible. A client of ours employed a dancing taco suit to great success for special events at his Tex-Mex restaurant.

In my very early marketing career, I also managed a karate school to make a little extra money. The school was located on one of the busiest streets in the city. To draw a little extra attention to the school, during the summer I used to hold class outside in the parking lot near the street. As traffic drove by they were drawn to rows of students dressed in their white pajama-like uniforms (called a gi), performing punches and kicks in unison while screaming at the top of their lungs with each move. I got my black belt in marketing long before karate!

One of my favorite No-B.S. Marketer stories is about a business that was running a huge ad campaign for a special event. To make their location easy to find, they had a huge, inflated blue balloon for consumers to use as a landmark. You could see it for miles. They ran a lot of media about the event, and each spot was tagged to "look for the big blue balloon." A competitor down the street, on the day of the event, flew his own blue balloon that was even bigger. Who do think got the biggest ROI on that deal?

## Email, Voice Mail, Phone, and Fax

In the new world order of marketing, there are many new buffers to keep your marketing message from reaching the intended, targeted potential customer. Email, voice mail, and faxes can all be incorporated into the mix of No B.S. Grassroots Marketing. Voice mail is a major issue for many businesspeople trying to reach their target audience. You have a much better chance of getting someone to return your message if you know some key secrets.

Renee Grant-Williams is the voice coach to the stars. Based in Nashville, she tutors such notables as Faith Hill, Tim McGraw, Christina Aguilera, Huey Lewis, and many others. She is the author of *Voice Power: Using Your Voice to Captivate, Persuade, and Command Attention*. The techniques that she uses to get these performers to maximize their star quality on stage and in recordings can also be used by businesspeople to make an impact on voice mail and even live phone calls.

Renee suggests that a quick, effective message is a great time saver. She says your goal in leaving the message should bring you one step closer to the person and the conclusion of business together. Leaving the "right" message depends on both content and delivery. The following steps will help you leave a professional message that increases your chance of getting your call returned.

### *Be Prepared*

Instead of just seeing voice mail as a chance to leave your name and number, see it as a way to advance your cause. You have one or at the most two opportunities to make a recorded impression. You can't afford to wing it.

- *Clearly state your information.* Following a brief benefit statement, leave your name, company, and telephone number. Say your telephone number clearly, allowing the other person enough time to write it down. Use your full name to identify yourself, and it is stronger to say, "This is so-and-so" rather than "My name is."
- *Ask for a specific action.* Rather than just asking someone to call you back, make a specific request. This allows the person to leave you the information you need, if you miss the return call.
- *Follow up your initial call.* You can call back without being labeled a pest. Let the person know that you understand how busy they are. Saying, "If you're not able to get back to me, I'll try to catch you next week," gives the other person an out. Also, if you are leaving several messages, keep notes on what you said during previous calls. You want your messages to sounds fresh and spontaneous.

- *Know when to stop talking.* Don't ramble just because you haven't been cut off. Remember, you are taking up someone's time. Your message will be appreciated if it is brief and to the point.
- *Adjust your attitude.* Even though you are talking to a machine, you need to speak to the person. The tone of your voice should reflect the content of your message. If you want to convey an upbeat attitude, smile. It will be heard in your voice.
- *Script your response.* I suggest you script out your message because it is too important to leave to chance. Remember, you only have a few seconds before the prospect decides to delete your message, so think of your first sentence as the headline of an ad or the opener to a radio commercial. Grab their attention with a benefit. Then follow up with your details, such as your name, company, and phone number. Repeat your phone number and slow down to give them time to jot it down.

Notice that the first sentence is a benefit statement. Create a statement that tells your prospect the end result of having used your product or service.

Usually, I'll leave no more than two voice mail messages; any more than that and you'll be perceived as a pest. One may get deleted prematurely, so the second attempt is fine. After the second message, I'll try to find out from the secretary or receptionist when's a good time to catch the prospect in. Sometimes, when requested, a secretary will give you a prospect's email address.

### From the Mouth of Babes

If nothing I try works, then I have to get a little creative. That's when I use a simple idea that was taught to me by my friend, Orvel Ray

Wilson, the co-author of *Guerrilla TeleSelling*. I get my son, Mitchell, on the phone to leave the message for me. He'll say, "Mr. Smith? This is Mitchell Slutsky. My Dad, Jeff Slutsky's been trying to get ahold of you for a while. And he said that he would take me to Disney World just as soon as you return his call." Well, do you think it worked? So far this year alone I owe my son 14 trips to Disney.

## An Exit Strategy That Helps Bring in Your Competitor's Orphaned Customers

When one or more of your competitors goes out of business, dramatically increase your business with a "competitive exit" program. Here are a few tactics that businesses have used successfully.

### *Get the Old Phone Number*

If a competitor of yours has closed their doors in the last several years (and did not sell it to someone else), consider getting their old phone number. To see if that number is available, call it. If you get a recording stating the number is out of service, your next step is to call your local service provider to see if they can get you that number. Joe Sheneman of Home Town Appliance did this and told us it cost them less than $30 a month. The old number is simply forwarded to their own number. In the first month, they noticed an average increase in their inbound call activity of 15%. The reason is that the old competitor still has an address and phone sticker circulating with that phone number and perhaps even has a Yellow Pages ad somewhere (once it's published, it could be out there at least as long as the book lasts).

### *Ask for the Referral*

If the old number is currently being used by a noncompetitive business or person, you can offer to buy the number from them for a year or so. Pay for the extra phone line so that the number can be forwarded to your business. If they don't want to do that, you might suggest that they'll probably be getting calls for your type of business. Tell them you would appreciate if they would give your number when they get those wrong numbers. Then offer to buy them a nice dinner or something for their effort. Sometimes these arrangements can be made directly with the receptionist.

If there is a delay because the number has not been released yet, you can do what Bob did for his Cincinnati sewing machine dealership. He called the former owner and offered him $100 to call the phone company on his behalf, for an intercept message. This way when a customer called the old number, instead of hearing that it's disconnected, the customer hears that the number has been changed. The new number in the message is Bob's.

### Buy the Customer List

A former competitor's mailing list can be a very valuable asset for someone still in the business. Offer to buy the list. Even if the list is a little out of date, it still could provide you with more new customers. Do a series of mailings to that list. Make sure the first mailing is first class so that you can get the returns of the bad addresses and can clean it up for future mailings.

### Put Up a Banner

"This company is out of business, but if you're looking for someone to take care of your needs, call our number." That's the approach a tire dealer outside of Denver used when his competitor vacated a building across the street. He got permission from the landlord, for a small fee, to put up a banner for a few months, with his address and phone, that stated he'd honor all the old business's tire warranties.

### *Mirror Their Advertising*

If the competitor ran an ad consistently over the years, run your ad in the same place and at the same times. Style your ad similarly to the old competitor's, but with your information.

## Clever Phone Numbers Help Ring Your Bell

Words are worth a thousand phone numbers. Spelling out a key word will make it easier for your customers and prospects to remember your number. For example, advertisements for Able Roofing feature their number, 444-ROOF. Atlas Butler Heating and Cooling likewise features their service in their number: 800-FURNACE. Nationally, companies including 1-800-Flowers and 1-800-Mattress not only made the number memorable; they named their company after it. Another great example is Hooked on Phonics: 1-800-A-B-C-D-E-F-G. Not to be outdone, we also decided to take advantage of this clever marketing tool by securing 1-800-SLUTSKY. Nobody else wanted that number so we grabbed it! Another benefit from using our name in our 800 number is that we also get extra publicity. In most interviews, speakers and authors usually don't get an opportunity to give out their contact information because it comes off being too commercial. But in many interviews I'm usually given a lead-in when the interviewer makes fun of my last name. When he does, I can launch into a routine about growing up with the last name of "Slutsky," and it ends by saying it's even my 800 number.

### *What's Your Number?*

When you're looking to get a memorable phone number for your business, here are a few tips to help you leverage this valuable marketing tool:

- *Incorporate it in all of your advertising.* Include this number in all your advertising, letterhead, on vehicles, and everywhere your company name appears. Think of it as an extension of your company name.

- *Make sure you buy similar numbers.* With all vanity numbers, there can be confusion around converting letters to numbers. If available, secure similar numbers or numbers that are frequently misdialed to reach you. Able Roof not only has 444-ROOF but also 444-ABLE, and 444-7003. Why the last one? Because sometimes people misread the "O" as a zero. Before they bought the 7003 number, they were losing around 300 calls per month. With our number, we reserved it with the last digit as a "4" instead of a "9" because people often spell "SlutskY" as "SlutskI."

- *Incorporate your number as your URL address.* If you already have a memorable number, turn it into an address on the World Wide Web. This has been done very successfully, for example, with www.1800flowers.com.

- *Spell out the number.* While a mnemonic number is memorable, the caller still must convert the letters to numbers. Make it easy for them. After your word number, in parentheses, italics, or a smaller type, place the numeric version. We do this in all our promotional pieces: 1-800-SLUTSKY (800-758-8759). However, if your ad or letter is asking for an immediate phone call, place the numerical number first, followed by the word number.

- *Get creative when looking for a memorable number.* For a local number it's best to use a four-letter word, unless the exchange spells out your word perfectly in seven letters. On toll-free numbers, you want to use seven-letter words. Write down a number of four-letter and seven-letter words that describe your business. Then see if those numbers are available. Perhaps 800-SHINGLE would also be a good number for a roofing company or an infectious disease clinic. Local numbers that spell HEAT or COOL might be great for an HVAC company. A number ending in 5325 (LEAK) could be used by a plumber or even an urologist. There are a lot of possibilities.

- *If possible, avoid words with the letters "O," "I," or "L." "O"* and "I" could easily be confused with "zero" and "one." The letter "L" can also sometimes be confused with the number "one."

## Email Is Free Mail

Email communications can provide you with an effective way to market to people as long as your message isn't perceived as spam. When sending regular mail doesn't reach your prospect, sometimes email can do the job for you. As with regular mail, you must have a credible list. So when you capture a contact's name, mailing address, and phone number, be sure to always ask for their email address, too.

The advantages of email over regular mail are obvious:

1. There's no cost of postage;
2 It's instant;
3. It's interactive and allows an immediate response;
4. You can send to as many addresses as you want with one click of the mouse.

Consider using email in conjunction with regular mail and other messaging means. Some customers prefer getting your information via email, while others prefer it in other formats. The more options you have, the more likely you are to reach the largest number of your customers with your message.

In an email, your "regarding" or "subject" line is like the headline in an advertisement. You want to write one that will beckon the recipient to open your email instead of hitting the delete key.

Don't abuse the privilege. Make sure that every time you email someone that you provide real value in the message. Failing to do so will get your emails blacklisted.

The format of your email can take several approaches. It can be as simple as a text message or as elaborate as an e-newsletter complete with photos, graphics, and even animation. The format you choose depends on your objectives and your budget.

Since you're relying on the recipient to open your email, it's best used with people who are already aware of you and have expressed interest in receiving your messages.

### E-zine

Renee Grant-Williams uses email to send out a monthly electronic newsletter to approximately 3,000 singers, speakers, and related businesses. She calls it the NewsFlash. Her NewsFlash is created in HTML format with the help of DreamWeaver and delivered via an autoresponder so it comes through as a web page, in full color, with links, photographs, and animation. Each page of her website (www.MyVoiceCoach.com) has a link with a free token gift to entice people to sign up to receive the NewsFlash, adding to the number of recipients daily. The tangible results are an increase of unique visitors to her website of 107% since her first issue. This has helped increase sales of her books, audios, and video products through her website by 154%.

### Use a Signature Line to Make It Easy to Contact You

Make sure to put all of your contact information in your automatic signature line to appear at the bottom of all your emails. Always make it easy for people to get back in touch with you by whatever means is most convenient for them. If possible, include your company logo as well. However, be careful with graphics because they could slow down the process or even get flagged as spam. When sending a generic email to a number of people in your address book, use the blind copy function (BCC) so that email addresses are not shared without permission.

## Just the Fax

The fax machine can be a powerful alternative or supplement to using emails and voice mails. One of the most successful uses of the fax machine I've tried was suggested to me by Hal Becker, author of *Can I Have Five Minutes of Your Time?* When I have a prospect that had expressed serious interest in our services but stopped returning my efforts to contact him, I send him a fax that reads:

Dear _____:

I've had a difficult time getting in touch with you to get your feedback about bringing me in to keynote at your annual convention. Please choose one of the options below and fax it back to me right away so I know where we stand.

(Please check one and fax back form.)

_____ I am ready to do the paperwork now.

_____ I'm still hashing things out. I'm busy now so please contact me on: (please give a convenient date and time) _____.

_____ I'm not interested. Please don't call again. Remove my name from your list.

This fax gets a very good response. I've gotten about a 50% response rate from it. Of the responses, they are almost equally divided among the three options.

### *Broadcast Fax*

Unsolicited broadcast faxes are annoying and illegal in most states. They are effective when the recipients have opted in to receive your fax. I used that method successfully by faxing a monthly article to our clients and prospects. Marc and I were writing a weekly column anyway for Knight Ridder, so it was easy to change the format to a fax sheet. It was sent out at the same time as the article was sent to the Knight Ridder/Tribune News Service to a list of people who wanted to receive an "advance copy" of the article. It was a great way to stay in touch with lots of people inexpensively. And since we were already doing the article, it didn't take much time. We also emailed the same article. The recipient would choose which way they preferred to receive the weekly article.

You can use the same approach to give your preferred customer advance notice of special offerings. But always give them the option to be removed from that list.

## Throw Combinations at Them

Prospects are all different and they respond uniquely to all forms of communications. Communicating by telephone and leaving voice mail may work better for some while fax or email work better for others. In the long term, however, you may want to use a combination of all of these to make the strongest impact. Add a few clever postcard mailings and you can develop a campaign that will allow you to determine which combinations provide the best return on your investment.

CHAPTER 12

# Publicity
## Free Advertising Brought to You by Your Local News Media

Jeff Slutsky

etting local publicity is part of any grassroots marketing solution. It can make more impact than advertising because it's not advertising. Your story becomes part of the entertainment, which is the reason people read the publication, listen to the radio, or watch the TV show. One downside of publicity, however, is that you have to aggressively go after it. Unlike advertising, you can't simply write a check and you're on the air or in print. You have to sell the media on the newsworthiness of your story. Reporters are not interested in giving you free exposure. However, they are interested in stories that would be of interest or value to their audience.

# NO B.S. GRASSROOTS MARKETING INCONVENIENT TRUTH #10

There is no such thing as 'off the record.' If you don't want your comments to end up on the front page of your local paper or media website, don't say it.

—Jeff Slutsky

The other downside is that you have no control over the content of the news item that is being printed or produced about you. There's always the possibility that getting publicity could backfire if the reporter sees something that is not positive about your business.

But given those negatives, the advantages are powerful. For more local business, you should look at local publicity as just one more piece of the puzzle. You can't rely on it to fully promote your business. But it can give your overall marketing program a nice boost from time to time.

One of the first things you need to do is decide if you're going to do the publicity yourself or hire a PR firm. A good, local PR firm will likely have some good contacts with the local media. They will likely be able to place stories more easily than you could yourself. For this, they'll charge a fee. This could either be a monthly retainer or a per-placement charge. Regardless of how they charge, you need to evaluate the return on your investment not by how much free press you get; rather, by how much business the free press creates for you.

PR firms like to have you evaluate them based on the value of the placement compared to regular advertising. If you get an article in your local daily newspaper that covers one-third of a page, they evaluate it as if you had purchased a one-third-page advertisement. From that perspective it's very fair, because in most cases an article should have significantly more impact thanan equivalently-sized ad.

However, what you really need to do is track your results like you should for any marketing program. Then, take the amount of business or profit you generated as a result of all the exposure the PR firm created, and subtract their fee and any other expenses related to that publicity to arrive at a return on your marketing investment. Just because you get a full-page article or a three-minute feature on the early and late news doesn't mean the exposure has paid for itself.

For most local businesses it should be relatively easy to work a simple publicity program into their operations. As in other local marketing efforts, if you spend a little time upfront to create a marketing infrastructure, you'll be prepared when the opportunity arises for you to inform the media of a possible news item.

Your first step should be to identify all the publicity outlets in your marketplace that are most appropriate for your business. The reality is that without this advance work, you might not get the time to suggest the story and you'll lose an opportunity for good, free publicity.

In addition to the news outlets, you want the names of the reporters or contacts for the various departments or specialties. For each of these contacts you want their mailing address, and if possible, their direct phone line and their personal email address. It would also help if you knew how they liked to be contacted (i.e., phone, mail, or email).

There are a lot more news outlets than you think. In addition to your major daily newspaper, there are suburban papers, and you probably have several specialty weekly publications geared for business, parents, kids, singles, religious and ethnic groups, association and organization newsletters, plus several monthly and quarterly magazines. In addition to the major TV networks, there are probably some cable opportunities. And with TV stations, in addition to their news rooms, there may be specific programs that could provide you an opportunity. Most radio stations will have newsrooms, but double-check to see if several stations are sharing a news department. Lastly, look for internet opportunities as well. Nearly every news outlet also has an internet outlet as well, so even if they don't want the story for their traditional news channel, they may use it on their website. And, you may find some local websites with opportunities in your marketplace.

With your major daily newspaper, you'll want to have a list of the appropriate editors of the various sections. You have the "city desk" for the basic news, business editor, arts and leisure editor, religious editor, home and garden editor, and so on. When you come up with a news story you should think about which editor would most likely be interested in it. Or you may want to slant your story or create an "angle" to a specific editor so that you're not inundating one editor all the time. A fundraising event for a church group at your location, for example, could be slanted to either the business editor or the religion editor. If they were raising money to revamp the landscape of their church, there might even be a lawn and garden angle as well.

Part of this research may already be available in some form. Check to see if there is a PR directory for your marketplace. You can get a lot of this information searching on the web as well. It could also be a nice project for a local college student working on a journalism or PR degree. This list will need to be updated from time to time, since reporters seem to move around a lot.

Next, determine the best way to reach each one. Email is becoming the preferred method of contacting most reporters and editors. This makes your job that much easier. If your story idea is very timely and possibly the making of a major feature story, you can even follow up with a phone call.

## Leverage Your Publicity

Once you get some publicity, you want to extend the value of it beyond the original exposure you got. With permission you can reprint the items that appeared in print. They can be framed or enlarged to put in your place of business. This allows your existing customers to see what you've done as well, and hopefully build a little more loyalty. If you get interviewed on the radio, get a recording of it and use it for a while with your "message on hold" on your phone system.

## Easy Ways to Generate Your Publicity

There are several ways to generate publicity. First, you can report on events that are happening already. A grand opening, new manager, title promotion, introduction of a new product or service, and charity fundraiser are all examples of business events that might be of interest to the right reporters. It may not get you a full feature story, but even a mention in another article or a small "blurb" helps.

The other way to generate publicity is to create an event specifically to capture the attention of the news media. For TV interviews you can have someone take pictures of you being interviewed and create a flier of the event. If the TV picture is good enough, you can even convert some TV images to print as well. You can use excerpts from all your publicity in your brochures or other promotional items. For example, we were featured in *Inc.* magazine with the headline, "Brains Over Bucks." So we use that quote along with the *Inc.* magazine name under it in many of our promotional pieces. It's simple and powerful.

But the most dramatic example of how powerful a news story can be came when I was featured in *The Wall Street Journal.* My company was not quite three years old and I was a one-man shop, struggling for survival. I knew I had something unique to offer to clients, but my No-B.S. Marketer concepts were a far different approach to marketing than most businesspeople were used to.

At the time I had a relationship with S & S Public Relations in Chicago. I had interned for Steve Simon who taught me a great deal about working with the news media and getting stories placed. S & S would do my PR for me in exchange for me training their newest account executives, who would be assigned to my account. So, in effect, I was the account supervisor for my own business. It was a great arrangement.

We did the normal types of PR stuff. I would help the new AE develop the press release, the press kit, and the list of targets, which included all the major business publications. Then I would help her learn how to follow up with the various reporters by telephone. This approach got various interviews on radio stations around the country and features in *The Chicago Sun Times, Nation's Business,* and a host of trade journals and dailies. Some of the stories would generate a phone call or two, but not much in actual sales.

Then I hit the equivalent of the journalistic Powerball. *The Wall Street Journal* called. A reporter by the name of Frank James working out of the Chicago bureau interviewed me. Then he called back several times to get details from the interview. He then checked out every story I gave him. It was the most difficult interview I'd ever been through. Finally Frank called me and said the story would run sometime the following week.

I was very excited. I knew that a paragraph or two in *The Wall Street Journal* would definitely bring me some clients. Tuesday night, I received a phone call from a guy who lived on my dorm floor at Indiana University. He said that he worked for *The Wall Street Journal* in Wisconsin, and his job was layout of the pages for the paper. He told me that my story would be in Wednesday's paper, on the front page of the second section. It included a sketch of me, and the article started at the top of the page and went down the entire page, one column wide, and finished deeper in the section.

This was exciting. I couldn't ask for better placement. I knew this would generate some business. I made a point of setting my alarm to get up at 8:00 so I could prepare for the phone calls. At this time, I was working out of my home office. The phone started ringing at 6:00 A.M.! As soon as I would hang up, it rang again. This went on until 10:00 that night. Most of the calls were sales of my audio album, and some were inquiries about seminars and speeches. The same thing happened the next day. Each successive day, there would be less inbound calls, but those calls came in solid for three months. Even after that, I'd get a call at least once a week for up to a year afterward; one lead turned into a six-figure consulting contract.

You would be lucky to get this type of PR once in a lifetime, but if you don't have a regular PR effort as part of your grassroots marketing solution, you'll never have the opportunity.

## Handling a PR Crisis

We were promoting one of our seminars. We had the support of the local chamber of commerce in that city and provided a special "member-to-member" discount to the chamber members. To help market the event to its members, the chamber provided us an email list of nearly 2,000 addresses and permission to send our message to them. What had started out as an economical marketing program turned into a marketing nightmare.

We first noticed a problem that evening when we started getting "mailer demons" every few seconds. Within an hour, there were over 500 emails to our address. Apparently there was a virus and a hacker that caused our email to be replicated repeatedly to everyone on the list. Not only was our email account getting overloaded, so were the other 2,000 people on that list. Each one of them thought they were getting hundreds of emails from us. There were some angry people, to say the least.

This is a classic marketing crisis situation. The problem was totally out of our control, yet we were getting all the negative PR. So we immediately went into crisis mode and identified the problem.

### *Develop a Response*

We started getting phone calls. Since the email originally went out on a Friday night, we actually got calls from people at our home on Saturday. In a line of defense, we had to script what we would say:

1. We are aware of the problem.
2. We apologize for the inconvenience.
3. Please understand that these emails are not coming from us.
4. We're doing what we can to solve the problem.

We made sure that everyone answering the phones followed that format. Plus, no matter the tone of the caller, receptionists were to be pleasant and apologetic. Of the many dozens of calls we received, the vast majority of the people, once we explained the situation, understood it and were empathetic. We also changed the outbound message of our voice mail to explain the problem. Once the inbound calls slowed down to a trickle, we changed the outbound message back to the original message.

The next step was to try to fix the problem at the source, if it's fixable. We called AOL, who started an investigation for us. We also contacted our IT provider to see if they could figure anything out. Next we contacted the chamber of commerce. They, too, received many phone calls. We explained the situation to them and they, like everyone else, were very understanding. They offered to send out a brief article explaining the situation in their weekly newsletter.

The last step was to make sure it would never happen again.

## Local PR

As a grassroots marketer, don't overlook the power of local publicity. Once you get into the habit of contacting your local media with newsworthy items, you eventually become a local expert in your community on your subject matter. Quotes and blurbs might not drive in big sales for you but they do help to create free awareness, exposure, and credibility in your marketplace. PR does not replace your other grassroots marketing approaches but makes a great supplement to your marketing plan. And every once in a while you might just get that PR grand slam feature story that blows off the doors to your customers!

# CHAPTER 13

# Come One, Come All to Your Marketing Event
## How to Get or Multiply Large Numbers of Customers at Blinding Speed

Dan Kennedy

I am a big fan of selling one to many, rather than one to one.

I also like getting people physically together, as nothing seems to trump the dynamic results that can be achieved with a good stage presentation and a live audience, but selling one to many via media is fine, too. The boardwalk pitchman who sold kitchen gadgets to small gathering crowds—an early career of Johnny Carson's sidekick Ed McMahon and the place the legendary TV pitchman Ron Popeil started—migrated to TV, first to infomercials, then to home shopping channels like QVC and HSN, and now to YouTube and video presentations at individual websites. In a lot of B2B situations as well as some consumer situations, great use can be made of teleseminars and webinars. All of that is beyond the scope of a single book, let alone a single chapter, so I'm going to stick to the physical-world event typically put on by or for a local business. Most of the principles apply to events held in cyberspace or on broadcast media as well.

## Selling Once to Groups in Events

Chiropractors, dentists, and other health-care professionals often advertise and conduct public health seminars or, more often, promote in-office "mini-seminars" to their own patient lists as well as accumulated leads from their websites and email opt-ins or social media. In the chiropractic field, my client, Dr. Chris Tomshack, CEO of HealthSource, with over 350 franchised clinics all across the country, has at least two in-office mini-seminars focused on different health topics, to which patients bring family members and friends. The doctor limits the seminar attendance to between a dozen or two dozen people, and frequently gets several new patients each time—patients committed to multi-thousand-dollar treatment programs for chronic pain management or for weight loss. Another client, Dr. Charley Martin, a very successful, candidly very expensive (but worth it!) dentist, conducts in-office mini-seminars for potential cosmetic and implant patients, and routinely creates upwards of $50,000.00 in work from one small class.

Restaurant owners who offer membership programs following a model taught to them by Glazer-Kennedy Insider's Circle invite customers to special appetizer or wine-tasting receptions and deliver a presentation to that group about their clubs, often signing up 50% or more of those in attendance.

Well-known companies like Tupperware—brilliantly run by its dynamic CEO, Rick Goings—use party-plan selling today very much the same way as in the 1950s, when my mother would attend Tupperware or Stanley Home Products parties. But did you know that Harley-Davidson sells motorcycles to women with "garage parties"? Home-party selling is a grassroots activity by its very nature: The sales agent leverages the hostess's family, friends, and neighbor list, and usually invitations are issued by phone and personal contact and may be extended friend to friend. A lot of local businesses with happy customers could use this business model, but it never occurs to them. A restaurant, winery, bakery, or gourmet foods shop owner could have a customer host an in-home tasting party, and there sell discounted gift cards, gift baskets, or products. A garden center owner could have a customer host a backyard garden party, give lessons in some sort of gardening and sell gift cards, products, and services.

Financial advisors rely heavily on free public seminars, workshops, and similar events to introduce themselves to prospective clients. I do a lot of work with about 60 such advisors from all over the country, probably bringing more than 150,000 people a year into financial information events. Much of the marketing in the industry for such events is very bland and relies on the lure of a free dinner at a country club, and advisors suffer with very poor response percentages from direct-mail invitations and often, poor-quality prospects. We use a very different approach, with multimedia and an emphasis on referral activity with existing clients, and rarely use free meals as a lure, preferring to bring people to the meetings for the right reasons: notably sincere interest in the subject matter. If you would like to see examples of our kind of financial advisor seminar marketing, you can do so free of charge at www.MattZagula.com and at www.CreatingTrustBook.com.

At events like these, at some point, there is and needs to be a sales presentation and a call to action, whether to purchase a product or book an appointment. I have been a professional at speaking to sell in such environments, to audiences of 30 to

30,000, for some 35 years, and for many years did so much of it, I earned a seven-figure yearly income just from my speaking and selling from the stage, and I've trained hundreds to do the same. I've written a complete special report on the subject of speaking to sell, which you can request and receive at www.NoBSBooks. com/free. Also, my book about the use of humor in speaking and selling, *Make 'Em Laugh and Take Their Money,* is available from booksellers. Jeff also addresses some of these same points in his book, *The Toastmaster's Guide to Successful Speaking,* available on Amazon.com. A caution: there is little point in doing these events if you are squeamish about the selling part, or unskilled and unwilling to get good at it. Just about anybody can get "good enough" to get results at the local level, but you can't take it for granted.

Of a less direct-selling nature, just about any and every business can effectively use and profit from customer appreciation events designed for customers plus family members, friends, and neighbors they invite. Positioned as a genuine thank you, and usually as entertainment, these events can introduce lots of potential customers to your business. One of our Glazer-Kennedy Insider's Circle members who does this brilliantly owns a family dairy farm, dairy store, and home-delivery business in Idaho. Alan and Holly Reed host Farm Days every year, with free hamburgers and hot dogs, a big picnic area, $.50 ice cream cones, music, hay rides, pony rides, cow milking contests, and more. The year I attended as an observer, about 3,000 people came through—two-thirds were present customers, and one-third, prospective customers. Without being heavy-handed about it, they capture guests' contact information for follow-up, and do have a way for guests to sign up on the spot for home delivery if they're on any of the company's routes. The Reeds gain hundreds of new customers each year using this grassroots marketing tactic.

My friend Ben Glass of GreatLegalMarketing.com guides many of the lawyers he coaches into grassroots efforts with various kinds of events. Shown in Figure 13.1 on page 196 is a notice in Mark and Alexis Breyer's client newsletter about their client and community appreciation dinners. As you can see, they are held at four different locations, on different dates, all around Phoenix, Arizona. Another of Ben's member-attorneys, Jason Epstein, in Bellevue, Washington, has his own community activism organization, Teens Against Distracted Driving, which arranges school programs to caution teens against dangerous driving habits, such as texting while driving.

Most of these kinds of events—other than pure home parties—tend to be promoted with media, whether internally only, i.e. to current and past customers and accumulated leads, or internally plus externally, i.e., via paid advertising in newspapers, on radio, on TV, etc., and use of online media. But they have a grassroots feel to them, and many are aided by the grassroots activities—the business owner being interviewed on local radio, news releases getting picked up by community newspapers, even broadsheets posted on restaurant and public bulletin boards. Some can be done under the auspices of schools, churches, community colleges, or civic groups.

## Do's and Don't's of Promotional Events

Now that you have an overview of how promotional events can be used to grow interest in your business, here are some tips we have collected from our experience.

- Never assume good attendance just because of goodwill. Events need to be marketed.
- Allow ample time for a good marketing effort. At a local level, this usually requires no less than three weeks to as much as eight weeks.

**FIGURE 13.1:** Mark and Alexis Breyer's Client Newsletter

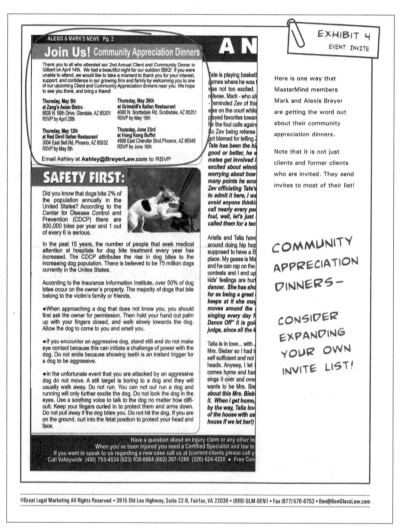

- Get people to pre-register, not just to show up at the door, so you can put them into a "keep 'em excited," reminder sequence of mailings, email, tweets, etc. If your prospects or customers will register online, the confirmation and follow-up emails can be entirely automated.

- If you are holding the event somewhere other than your own place of business, give a lot of consideration to that location. A convenient, known, or easy-to-find location, safety, and ample free parking are all critical. It shouldn't be too fancy for your crowd, but not bargain-basement either—people want to come to a nice place.

- I'm very big on theme-park thinking, and have used all sorts of themes—including a Desert Cruise (in Arizona), complete with bon voyage party, hotel made over as a cruise ship, captain's cocktail party; an Under-the-Big-Top Three-Ring Circus with all those trappings; Build a Better Business construction-themed events, with rented earth movers and bulldozers parked outside, hard hats for everybody, and sexy "Tool Time Girls," wearing hard hats and tool belts, as greeters; and on and on. For the small, local event, you obviously can't go to the extremes and expense that I and my clients do with an international conference, but I still suggest using a theme and going as far as you can. Make your event sound fun, unusual, and interesting.

- If the emphasis is on delivery of information, that must be made not just interesting but exciting and timely. Again, you can see examples of how we do this in the financial advisory field at www.MattZagula.com and at www. CreatingTrustBook.com. The number one marketing sin is being boring. You need to generate some tabloid-like sensationalism around what people are going to discover as well as why they need to know about it, now. Emphasize the promise of benefit or gain just from attending. And the speaker(s) need to be made as interesting, authoritative, and given as much celebrity as possible.

Sometimes the value of business to be gained warrants serious investment in a unique and extraordinary event. Jeff Slutsky described his work with a client group of regional pharmaceutical reps working for Bristol Myers-Squibb. To get the undivided, favorable attention of a group of doctors, they organized an evening of fine dining and entertainment. In face-to-face selling in the offices, a rep like these is lucky to get a fast five minutes, but they had four different drugs they wanted to present in some detail. This team of reps was able to get 100 doctors (and their spouses) to an evening featuring the singer LaDonna Gatlin, baby sister of the famed Gatlin Brothers, and comedian Steve Rizzo. The show began with about 30 minutes of LaDonna's regular stage performance followed by Steve's comedy and motivational material. But instead of boring technical explanations of the drugs, the grand finale was presented by LaDonna and Steve in parody songs! Jeff rewrote the lyrics to eight songs from the musical *The Sound of Music*, got them cleared by the company's legal department, and LaDonna and Steve performed them. To *The Sound of Music*: "The halls are alive with the sounds of mucus." To *Climb Every Mountain*: Claim Every Patient. And the crowd favorite about hypertension: You're 216 over 117. No, it won't win a Tony Award, but it did avoid the dreaded, dry technical speech by the corporate executive, and stayed true to the promise of an evening of entertainment.

Obviously, such an event ain't cheap. You need Jeff or somebody like him—and, really, is there anybody like him?—to conceptualize, create, organize, hire talent, secure music use rights, and also speak at the event. He and his creative partner Steve Rizzo are wizards at all this. In evaluating how elaborate and costly to get with your event, you have to consider two things: one, the value of the business as a whole and of each client to be gained; and two, all the costs associated with getting that business and securing those clients by other means. There is probably also a "buzz factor" for you beyond those in the audience and beyond the event itself. You can also consider videotaping it for subsequent use at your websites, on YouTube, and in DVDs used in direct-mail campaigns. Don't "knee-jerk" decide something like this is "too expensive." Think it through carefully.

In B2B environments, Jeff and I are both occasionally used as "drawing cards." A company hires him or me to speak at a seminar or even a teleseminar or webinar, to give them a high-value program as a gift to clients, get clients to bring guests, and to promote to new prospects. Speaking for myself, I'm not a cheap date. I fly by private jet, command a good day fee, and require bulk purchase of my books as attendee gifts and/or book sales. I do have a portfolio of ready-to-use, proven promotional material that can be customized for any client, which is of obvious value. I have been employed this way by various clients selling different services to chiropractors, dentists, small-business owners, and financial advisors. When you hire a speaker for such purposes, it's important that he or she be fully on board with your marketing objectives, not just showing up and delivering off-the-shelf shtick, and not putting your purposes at risk for his own. Furthermore, he or she has to be very promotable—either a famous celebrity who is relevant to your audience or someone of less fame but great authority and relevance—who your clientele can be motivated to be eager to hear.

Whether a high-value, educational program, or a mini off-Broadway production, you need to do some expert planning and very thorough promotion to leverage your investment.

If an event is free, your advertising for it needs to explain how it is being offered free of charge, even if very briefly, to allay skepticism and worry. This can be as simple as, "Sponsored by the Elder Law Center as community outreach," but it needs to be said. If nothing will be sold, you usually want to emphasize that. If something is to be sold, I usually prefer disclosing, gently, that there will be a brief commercial on behalf of "x," but also reassuring that beneficial information will be provided and a good time will be had by all.

Skepticism of free events can sometimes be allayed if the event is sponsored or tied to a charity. In B2B environments, my clients using free seminars that sell often get one or more noncompeting vendors to sponsor the events, and sometimes, also, underwrite some or even all of the costs. When I wanted to do free seminars as part of a nationwide book tour, I got the software company InfusionSoft to sponsor and host four events in four cities. Locally, a professional putting on an event could bring another noncompeting professional in to split time and cost and co-promote. Or, a charity tie-in might be created; an elder law attorney might, for example, affiliate his event with the local chapter of the Arthritis Foundation and make a donation based on attendance. Jeff did a similar program with an eight-city tour specifically for comic book retailers, which was sponsored by Marvel Entertainment.

Plan the event itself carefully. People need to be greeted, checked in, and ushered to the event area. If there is a wait time between arrival and the start of a program, they should be given something to look at; literature or an event program, and you may want to have a video showing in the room. At seminars that sell, for financial advisors, doctors, and others, we use five- to seven-minute video compilations of their media appearances, TV commercials, infomercials, and testimonials, and have that running back to back, again and again, during the wait time. The primary speaker should almost always be formally introduced to establish authority—even if you believe much of the audience is familiar with them.

## Large Numbers at Blinding Speed

For most businesses, nothing beats an event that gets current customers, clients, or patients to round up and bring family, friends, neighbors, and co-workers to be introduced to you.

Multiplying satisfied customers in this way can create exponential growth: iIf 20 customers each beget 2 via an event, there are 60 customers for the next event, times 2 equals 120, multiplied by 2 at the next event, gives you 240.

Another great way to get numbers and speed is by cooperative list sharing among merchants in an area for one big event. In many areas—including mine, where I saw it firsthand—all the merchants in a shopping village collaborated on a 7 P.M. to midnight Harry Potter night linked to the midnight release of the series' newest book. Every store and restaurant stayed open. Everyone had some Harry Potter-themed gift, trinket, or snack, so kids could go from one merchant to the next to the next, winding up at the bookstore. Kids came in costumes to get the book at a discount. It resembled a giant Halloween party, suggesting that could just as easily be pulled off as a theme. With every merchant at least using its email list to promote, some mailing, and in-store promotion for weeks in advance, everybody got the benefit of everybody else's reach. Customers also brought friends with their kids who may never have been to these shops before. The few shrewd enough to capture visitors' contact info created new prospect lists for follow-up. Many enjoyed a cash-flow surge and gained new customers. Mostly, independent bookstore owners organized these, but any merchant could be the organizer.

Jeff Slutsky is a master of the "blowout promotion"—usually a single day or weekend for a retailer or restaurateur—designed to generate an enormous amount of trial of your product or service in a very short time. It can get a lot of people familiar with a new business or a business in a difficult location in a hurry. It can restart a troubled business. And, as Jeff says, sometimes it is net-cheaper to acquire customers by just giving the product away free than by any other means. I have a client, KidsBowlFree.com, who represents a huge number of bowling centers all across the country, and uses their slowest times (days during the summer) as free and nearly-free gifts distributed to its list of over one million family members, bringing first-time customers into those centers.

Jeff describes a fairly typical blow-out promotion for a Luby's Cafeteria in Tampa, Florida:

"Their 'Customer Appreciation Day' featured an outrageous 50%-off everything. They brought in a banjo player, a magician, and a balloon artist to entertain guests, decorated the place to reinforce the festive spirit, and, of course, made sure they had enough food ready to support the promotion. Running out of product halfway through this kind of a promotion would be disastrous. Not only do you need enough product, you need enough labor to deliver excellent service. Luby's brought in general managers from other area Luby's to lend a helping hand and expose them to the possibilities of such a promotion. The power of a promotion like this is in getting many first-time customers—in this case, who might never otherwise venture into a cafeteria—to try your business. Since the price is so low, it's clear it's a one-time event, and you don't risk eroding price integrity. Sales tripled for the day and customer counts quadrupled. But the important fact is that store sales were up 13% for the month following the promotion. Approximately half those who came that day were new customers and the boost to sales the following month was testament to many returning. To get those same numbers of new customers over time through traditional advertising or couponing would cost significantly more money."

The way I would try to make this kind of an event even better, looping back to the Harry Potter example, would be to inveigle two noncompeting area merchants of one kind or another who had sizable email or mailing lists and trade them the equal of an exhibit booth with coupon and/or sample distribution inside the Luby's, right smack in the middle of all the activity, for promotion of the event in their name to their list. For a Luby's, it could be a window replacement company, a retail store, or a home services provider like a carpet cleaning company—or even a car dealer displaying their newest car in a velvet-roped area outside, adjacent to the entry. You could also go for a charity tie-in, making a donation for every meal served, in exchange for the charity's promotion of the event to its list. With a charity tie-in, you may find it easier to get free promotion on local radio and TV programs and in community newspapers. In short, I like using events as newly created opportunity for others, thus creating barter currency to exchange for access and endorsement to others' lists.

You can choose to utilize one of your slower days or times of the week, to avoid cannibalizing your peak sales times, although if this event is promoted in a big enough way it will admittedly cut into sales on the days leading up to it as people delay their visits or purchases to take advantage of the sale. In the case of a business like Luby's, though, that tradeoff is that they may bring friends who are potential new customers.

One vital point Jeff makes is it's of critical importance to distribute bounce-back certificates. This is the only real way to track how many of the participants in the day's promotion return as customers, and it encourages them to return, within a prescribed time period. The certificate can give a blanket, next-time discount, or a discount on certain items, or offer a gift with the next purchase, and it should bear an expiration date.

It might not occur to you that a good time to run this kind of blow-out promotion is immediately before a competitor's grand opening, but Jeff suggests it is. You'll take some of the wind out of their sails and diminish whatever success they may have at purloining your customers.

## When the Circus Came to Town, Everybody Went

If you're familiar with the great Barnum & Bailey or Ringling Brothers circuses, or have read the outstanding novel *Water for Elephants*, or watched the HBO series *Carnivàle*, you know that once upon a time in America, when the circus came to town, everybody went. This is no longer the case. The box in the living room and the iPad under the arm present a dizzying array of entertainment as well as educational "events" that do not require trudging off to a tent and paying admission. Personally, I never thought of it as "trudging" and I think much has been lost to families and society in general by the disappearance of shared, special experiences into the little electronic boxes, but that's another subject for another time and place. So, today, it takes a lot to motivate people to come to your event. Still, people go. And the putting on or participating in events is the most certain way to gain customers in clumps versus one at a time, with speed and efficiency. Every No-B.S. Grassroots Marketer should be using event promotions.

# The Wizard of Sales
### by Jeff Slutsky

With the success of the Bristol Myers-Squibb *Sound of Mucus* show and the National Speakers Association version of *Grease*, it became obvious to Steve Rizzo and me that we were on to something. Steve called me one day and asked me to write him a one-man show that he can do in addition to his standard keynote speech. Steve is a gifted impressionist, so the parodies can involve using his unique talents.

# The Wizard of Sales, continued

Both of us speak to a lot of sales organizations, so we agreed that the show should be geared to salespeople. But it should be general enough so that the basic framework of the show could be recycled, and then with a rewrite, adapted to the unique needs and issues of a given client. So it would be a custom show, but many of the most expensive elements of the show would be reusable to help make it cost effective for everyone.

I called Steve back two weeks later with good news and bad news. The good news was I already completed a rough draft of his one-man show. The bad news was that it took a cast and crew of 12 to perform it. That's when I suggested we do a parody of *The Wizard of Oz* for salespeople. First of all, not only does every person know all the music intimately, but everyone knows all the characters and the plot.

For our pilot version, the four main characters would have to overcome four basic selling issues that nearly everyone in a sales audience would identify with (see Figures 13.2 to 13.5 on pages 206–208). Dorothy will have a problem closing the sale. The Scarecrow can't generate good qualified leads. The Tinman will have a problem handling objections. And the Cowardly Lion (played by Steve Rizzo) will have telephone-call reluctance.

The way it's written, the production is both parody and sequel of sorts. Dorothy, after graduating from Kansas State University, gets a job as a sales rep. In her office are three other salespeople: Hunk, Hickory, and Zeke. The sales manager is Mr. Marvel. And her big competitor, who keeps stealing away her best sales, is Elmira Gulch.

# The Wizard of Sales, continued

After losing yet another sale to Elmira (this time because of price), she sings, "Somewhere over my sales goals." Throughout the production, each character learns to overcome their particular sales issue.

To ensure that the production was of the highest quality, Broadway director Michael Leeds staged and choreographed the entire production with the help of Broadway musical director Phil Reno. The costumes were designed by Tony Award winner Alvin Colt, who also did the costumes for Forbidden Broadway. His concept was to give each character the "business version" of their movie counterpart. Dorothy wears a blue gingham business dress. Hickory is in a stylish silver gray business suit which later turns into his tin business suit. Huck wears a sport coat and tie but is transformed into the Scarecrow, stuffed with shredded cancellation orders.

**Figure 13.2** The sales force before they're transformed.

# The Wizard of Sales, continued

The pilot performance was at the Marriott Marquis in New York City for the IRDC, a real estate trade group. Then the first full production was performed at the National Speakers Association annual convention in Washington, DC. In both cases the scripts were rewritten to address the needs and issues of the audience.

**Figure 13.3** Dorothy gets advice from Munchkin Corp. with the help of the Good Sales Manager of the East.

The template production is not limited to salespeople. It's designed to be rewritten for basically any audience. Of course, there needs to be enough lead time to research and write a script. Then the cast has to learn a new script each time, even though the blocking and choreography are mostly the same for each show. One interesting point is that the cast has no idea why a certain line is funny to the audience. I tell them where to anticipate a laugh or applause so they can pause accordingly.

# The Wizard of Sales, continued

**Figure 13.4** The "Great and Powerful Wizard" happens to look strangely like the president of the organization, but just a little greener.

**Figure 13.5** Tinman suffers from poor objection handling while Dorothy advises him with wisdom from The Ruby Sales Manual.

# The Wizard of Sales, continued

To pursue this kind of production for your event, be sure to look for very talented people who can deliver the final value for you. First find a writer who is not only funny, but understands business. You want someone who can research your business to the point of being an expert. Then he or she is ready to put it on paper for you. Try not to limit this person's creativity. If you want a show but it doesn't matter which music you use, let the writer choose, based on the audience. If you choose the music (unless there's a strategic reason it needs to something specific), your writer may not be able to give you the best results.

A good director is also important, especially one with "industrial" experience. The staging at most conventions has to be set up specifically for that event, so the production *is not working with the standard stage*. The show has to be adapted to work within the restrictions of the staging, or if possible, when the staging is being designed to allow elements that would make for a smooth production. The same goes for the lighting and the sound.

The sound is very important and seems to be the one area groups scrimp on. The entire show is based on the audience hearing the lyrics. Actors can wear wireless microphones with headsets, like they do on Broadway. But it's super important to make sure that you get a crisp, clear sound from those mikes, or the show is lost. To see a nine-minute promotional video on *The Wizard of Sales*, search on YouTube for Wizard of Sales or log on to YouTube and put this in your browser window: http://www.youtube.com/watch?v=K_I75X9uCg8.

# CHAPTER 14

# Profitable Espionage
## Data Mining, Intelligence Gathering, and Covert Operations

Jeff Slutsky

Your database of customers is perhaps the most valuable asset you have in your business. It is literally a diamond in the rough just waiting for you to discover those few precious marketing jewels within its bytes. A key to No B.S. Grassroots Marketing is to not only mine those rough nuggets of high value, but also learn how to refine your efforts.

Through the use of automated statistical analysis (or "data mining") techniques, businesses are discovering new trends and patterns of behavior that previously went unnoticed. Once they've uncovered this vital intelligence, it can be used in a predictive manner for a variety of applications.

In its very basic form, data mining can be as simple as the business-card drawing tactic mentioned in Chapter 6. That simple approach allows you to capture a large number of clients' valuable information. And of course, it's most applicable in a retail setting where you have a large customer base and generally don't get an opportunity to know your customers on a first-name basis.

The downside of this approach, of course, is the amount of time it takes to develop the database. However, there will soon be a variety of providers who will be developing databases like this for just about any group. The key is to use the information once you get it so you can generate a healthy return on your investment

The more focused your target list is, the more efficient you can be in contacting them. Mass mailing is tremendously inefficient, which is why 98% of it is tossed out. But with a stronger list, fully researched and indexed, you can afford to create messages more specific to the reader. You also can afford to send more elaborate pieces that would be cost prohibitive in a mass mail setting.

## The Most Profitable

One exercise we have clients do is to identify which segment of their customer base is the most profitable. This doesn't necessarily mean they're the highest volume buyers. And when we look at profitability we look at more than margin. We also look at how much of your internal resources are needed to properly service that account. So you may have an account that provides you good volume and decent margins, but takes up so much of your time in keeping them happy that the relationship becomes unprofitable.

The purpose of the exercise, of course, is to try to identify those traits of clients you would most like to replicate when looking for future clients. Instead of seeking any and all newcomers to your business, you can focus you marketing and sales efforts to a narrow target audience that provides you the best overall return on your investment, not just with the marketing costs, but also with the cost of maintaining that client.

Once you quantify those desirable characteristics, use your No-B.S. Marketer data-mining tactics to root out leads that closely emulate that segment of your customer base. For example, when we are prospecting for clients to sell a major neighborhood marketing sales project, we look to our previous client experience as a guide. The first piece of the matrix is the business model: chains, franchises, independents. Then there's the number of units in the marketplace. Next, we look at growth in both same store sales and new units. The type of client most likely to invest the necessary funds to develop and implement such a large project is a business that has both franchise and company-owned units where one or the other is at least 25% of the total.

If a company is showing a lot of growth in sales and is expanding a lot, it probably won't be willing to commit the resources, both financial and internal, to make a comprehensive neighborhood marketing program work for them. It's easier just to throw a bunch of money against the mass media to drive sales, regardless of its ROI. But when things slow down, franchisees complain that "corporate" isn't' doing enough; their mass-media advertising budget is maxed out; they need to do something dramatic to jump-start the organization. The company has to have a minimum of 50 units to begin to consider such a project and there needs to be a lack of market penetration with most of them. That is, there are not enough units located in a single ADI or DMA to consider the use of mass media in that market. Assuming the operational part of the business is still strong, we know we can make a big impact for them and, more importantly, that client is more likely to take our advice and not water down the program. That's not to say that other combinations within that matrix wouldn't be effective. It's that we know that this ideal matrix is easier to sell and easier to provide a strong ROI on our work.

The point is, instead of taking any business that happens to contact you, create a very specialized hit list and get creative and aggressive in going after it. In the meantime, if some low-hanging fruit happens to find its way to you, pluck it.

## *Data Capture*

The key to any successful data-mining program is the capture of the information from the customer. This needs to be done in a nonintrusive way as to not offend your customer. Again, the business card drawing is one nonintrusive example. If you want to capture information about your customer's home environment, you can still run a fishbowl drawing, but instead of using business cards, have your customers fill in an entry form. With an entry form, you can capture the specific information you want.

Keep in mind that if you start getting involved in too much detail on an entry form, your customers may not want to participate in your drawing. To help you in this area, consider the "long form" entry for your contest. This is where you present the possibility of winning a prize in your drawing. The entry form asks for the basic information: name, home address, phone, email, and perhaps age, birthday, place of work, or several other items. Then, on the form and also on the poster, state that the participant can "double the prize" by filling out the additional ten questions on the form. It's an option. The addition questions solicit some key information you are trying to capture.

Other areas of data capture include information available when someone writes you a check or pays by credit card. A car wash, for example could jot down the license numbers of the customers, and from that they can go online and glean information that way. There are services online that, for a small fee, can conduct background checks and gather valuable information on just about anybody.

You may get a number of inbound calls inquiring about your services, but callers are hesitant in giving you information. Caller I.D., if not blocked, gives enough information to get started. From that, you can track down a mailing address and market directly to that person without them realizing they've been targeted.

You do want to temper your desire to capture your customer's contact information with their willingness to give it. Your first priority should be to provide a positive buying experience. Then you capture the information provided it doesn't interfere with developing good customer relations.

---

# Data Capture Gone Wrong

My absolute favorite example of data capture gone wrong is told by my good friend Larry Winget, one of the most gifted personal development speakers and author of *It's Called Work for a Reason*. He shares this story:

> I was walking through the mall one day when I realized I needed to stop and buy some batteries. I saw a store in the mall I knew sold batteries, so I headed toward it. I pulled the batteries off the rack and laid the batteries on the counter along with my cash. A guy on the other side of the counter looked at me and said, "Can I have your name, address, and telephone number?" Have you ever had that happen? Of course you have. I said, "No." Want to start having some fun in life? Then just get good at saying no. Stores don't have any idea what to do when the customer just real politely says no.

---

# Data Capture Gone Wrong

*continued*

So the guy at the counter said to me, "Sir, we have to have your name, address, and telephone number in order to sell you the batteries." I asked him why. He then went on to tell me the number-one thing that no customer ever wants to hear. He said, "Sir, because that is our company policy." I told him I had a "customer policy" and that my customer policy was that for $1.79 worth of batteries, when I was paying cash, I didn't need to tell him who I was.

At that point, he pushed the batteries across the counter and said he wouldn't be able to sell me the batteries. I asked if there was a manager there. He told me the manager was in the back, but he would go get him. He then went in the back and came out with what I recognized right off to be a manager: It was a kid about 19 years old. You've seen this guy, haven't you?

The manager approached the counter with his finger pointed at me, stopped in front of me with that finger about a foot from my nose and said, "Sir, do you have a problem?"

I told him I didn't have any problem at all. He had batteries and I had money, and in America, we call that . . . a deal. He said, "You are going to have to give us your name, address, and telephone number, or we are not going to sell you the batteries." I explained it just wasn't going to happen. I knew he had a company policy but I had a customer policy. Besides, I told him I wanted him, as the manager, to explain to me why it was necessary to

# Data Capture Gone Wrong

*continued*

give all of my personal information when I was paying cash. He then told me the second thing no customer ever wants to hear: "Because that's the way we've always done it."

I told him I had really good news for him because on that day, he was going to get to find a way to do it differently.

At that point, he pushed the batteries across the counter at me and said, "We aren't doing business with you!" and turned to walk away. I said, "Listen, you are the manager and I am the customer. You should be able to figure out some way for me to get the product that I came in here for and, believe it or not, am still willing to pay for, so don't walk away until you at least stop and think about this for a minute."

He stopped, thought for a while, turned and walked over to his computer where he started to type. In just a minute, he took my money and handed me some change. Then he put the batteries in a bag along with a receipt that he pulled from his computer, saying to me, "There you go, I figured it out."

I asked him what he had figured out. He told me that he had just put his own name, address, and telephone number on my receipt.

Excerpted with permission from Larry Winget (www.larrywinget .com), author of the number-one bestseller, *Shut Up, Stop Whining & Get A Life!* and host of the A&E TV series *Big Spender.*

## Data Mining Your Competition

Next to your own customer database, the most valuable database you can get is that of your competitor. A pizza restaurant used to drive to the competition and write down the license plate numbers of the cars parked out front. Those numbers were converted to names and mailing addresses. It was compared against his own customer database. If there was a name that showed up on both databases, they received a moderate discount in the mail. If the name did not show up on his database, they received a big discount to motivate that customer for a first-time trial. The danger of this approach, of course, is if your customers find out what you're doing, it could create ill-will in the community. For that reason, I recommend great care.

Another approach I don't recommend but was successful nonetheless was done by a jewelry store with the help of a friend's health club. You've, no doubt, seen the boxes on countertops in different retail establishments offer a free health club membership. The customer of that restaurant or video rental place fills out the form and puts it in the box. The jewelry store owner had his buddy put those boxes in several of the competing jewelry stores around town. The prize to be drawn was a $50 gift certificate from the store that was permitting the box drawing. What they didn't know is that when the drawing was made, the health club owner gave the entry forms to his friend who owned the jewelry store. He now has a list of customers of his competition.

## Follow the Leader

Sometimes good business intelligence simply takes initiative. Consider the owner of a Kansas company that sold water treatment systems for homes. When his salespeople complained they did not have any good leads, he spent the better part of a day in an affluent neighborhood following the Culligan delivery truck around and writing down the addresses of each delivery. Using a crisscross directory he generated 50 leads of people who were already spending about $30 a month on filtered water. He explained to his sales people that their product would pay for itself in short order and the leads were out there if they were willing to work to capture the information.

One of my all-time favorite examples of data mining before the advent of the internet was used by Chuckles the Clown in Fort Wayne, Indiana. He would visit the "morgue" at the local daily newspaper and look at the birth announcements from five years earlier. His target audience was the parents of 5-year-olds who would use him for their birthday parties. With the names in hand he would develop a database with addresses and phone numbers from which he would market. Of course, the internet makes that type of activity easier to do now, but the idea is the same.

A similar approach can be used to create a list from "divorces granted." Three months later, that person would probably pay attention to advertisements for a dating service, teeth-whitening, and weight-loss programs. If you sell items that would make a great anniversary gift, you could work the same way. Focus on marketing to the husband, and be sure to cross-reference any anniversary dates you have with divorces filed or granted to make sure they're still together.

## A Grassroots Mentality

To succeed in your business, you need to take advantage of every legal means possible to gather and use information about your customers, your competition, and their customers. Information is power. If you can avoid costly mistakes of wasted marketing dollars or uncover some unique opportunity to zero in on a key target audience at a fraction of what you have paid in the past, you're on your way to truly becoming a No-B.S. Grassroots Marketer.

## No B.S. Grassroots Marketing Inconvenient Truths

### *No B.S. Grassroots Marketing Inconvenient Truth #1*

Advertising is not the only answer to a need for customers or sales. Advertising may not even be the best answer. Advertising relying on out-of-context of marketing fails more often than not. And the least effective advertising, shunned by consumers, is advertising lacking personal relevance to those customers.

Much disappointment, frustration, and failure can be traced to the fool's mission of finding a single, simple solution to a complex problem or opportunity.
—Dan Kennedy

• • •

### *No B.S. Grassroots Marketing Inconvenient Truth #2*

It doesn't make sense to promote your Yellow Pages ad in your other advertising. Why would you direct a potential customer to the only medium that puts you directly next to all of your competitors?

• • •

### *No B.S. Grassroots Marketing Inconvenient Truth #3*

More marketing dollars are wasted on local sponsorships than just about anything else. Unless you know how to leverage a sponsorship, you'll probably see no return on your investment. So unless your kid is on the team, don't waste your money.

• • •

### *No B.S. Grassroots Marketing Inconvenient Truth #4*
There is no substitute for REAL, personal,
person-to-person relationships.

• • •

### *No B.S. Grassroots Marketing Inconvenient Truth #5*
"Money Math" is NOT simple or easy. But getting it right
is essential to winning as a David against Goliaths,
to getting more productivity from
every invested dollar.

• • •

### *No B.S. Grassroots Marketing Inconvenient Truth #6*
If you can't track it, it don't hack it. Without tracking the
results of your marketing, you will never know how
to get the absolute most from your
marketing dollars.

• • •

### *No B.S. Grassroots Marketing Inconvenient Truth #7*
There are lots and lots and lots of things you can do with
advertising, marketing, and promotion, but just because
you can, doesn't mean you should. Do what you do for the
right reason. Be wary of investing in things because they
are popular, are normal and customary, are what "everybody"
does, "cool kids" do, or giants do. Be resistant to pressure by
media salespeople, marketing "gurus" biased to or selling
particular tools, and employees, peers, friends, and family.
Not everyone has your best interests in mind. Not
everyone with opinions has qualified opinions. It is

YOUR responsibility to hold each investment and
activity up to harsh assessment and measurement,
to minimize risks, avoid waste, and obtain
positive returns.

• • •

### No B.S. Grassroots Marketing Inconvenient Truth #8

Most local marketing programs fail not because of lack of good
ideas, but because of poor follow-through and support.
—Jeff Slutsky

Commitment is more important than creativity.
—Dan Kennedy

• • •

### No B.S. Grassroots Marketing Inconvenient Truth #9

Billboards are only useful if drivers can read them. Limit
the copy to no more than three elements, six words, clean
type, and a simple, easy-to-understand message.
If you can't do that, don't waste your money.

• • •

### No B.S. Grassroots Marketing Inconvenient Truth #10

There is no such thing as 'off the record.' If you don't want
your comments to end up on the front page of your local
paper or media website, don't say it.
—Jeff Slutsky

## Other Books by Dan Kennedy

### Other Books in the No B.S. Series by Dan Kennedy published by Entrepreneur Press

No B.S. *Business Success in The New Economy*

No B.S. *Sales Success in The New Economy*

No B.S. *Wealth Attraction (for Entrepreneurs) in The New Economy*

No B.S. *Direct Marketing for Non-Direct Marketing Businesses*

No B.S. *Marketing to the Affluent*

No B.S. *Ruthless Management of People & Profits*

No B.S. *Time Management for Entrepreneurs*

### New

No B.S. *Price Strategy* (with Jason Marrs)

### Coming Soon

No B.S. *Trust-Based Marketing* (with Matt Zagula)

No B.S. *Marketing to Seniors & Leading Edge Boomers* (with Chip Kessler)

### Other Books by Dan Kennedy

*Ultimate Marketing Plan* (4th Ed./20th Anniversary Edition) (Adams Media)

*Ultimate Sales Letter* (4th Ed./20th Anniversary Edition) (Adams Media)

*Uncensored Sales Strategies* with Sydney Barrows (Entrepreneur Press)

*Making Them Believe* with Chip Kessler (Glazer-Kennedy/ Morgan James)

*Make 'Em Laugh & Take Their Money* (Glazer-Kennedy/Morgan James)

*Unfinished Business/Autobiographical Essays* (Advantage)

*The New Psycho-Cybernetics* with Dr. Maxwell Maltz (Prentice-Hall)

**Book information @ www.NoBSBooks.com**

## Other Books and Videos by Jeff Slutsky

*Street Fighter Marketing for Your Business* (Lexington Books)
*Street Fighter Marketing Solutions* (Simon & Schuster)
*Street Smart Marketing & Selling: Innovative Tactics for Increasing Sales* (on DVD)

### With Marc Slutsky

*How to Get Clients* (Warner Books)
*Smart Marketing* (Career Press)
*Street Smart Marketing* (Wiley & Sons)
*Street Smart Tele-Selling: The 33 Secrets* (Prentice Hall)

### With Michael Aun

*The Toastmasters Guide to Successful Speaking* (Dearborn Publishing)

### With Larry Winget

*From the Big Screen to the Real World* (Win Publishing)

# Index

**A**

ad frequency, 56–58
advertising. *See also*
    marketing
    ad agencies, 14–15
    co-op advertising,
        15–16, 53–54
    effectiveness of, 1–4.
        *See also* tracking
        results
    immunity to, 48
    with mass media. *See*
        mass advertising
        media
    non-traditional, 11–12
    outdoor advertising,
        9–10, 24, 161–169
    on radio, 8–9, 55–58,
        61
    on television. *See* TV
        advertising
    traditional, 5–11
    in Yellow Pages,
        10–11, 62–64
advertising codes, 40–41
advertising pollution, 48
affinity anchors, 126
audits, local marketing,
    75–76

automated statistical
    analysis. *See* data
    mining
awareness builder
    program, 51

**B**

billboards, 166–168
blowout promotions,
    201–203
bounce-back certificates,
    201–203
branding, 4–5
broadcast faxes, 179
broadcast TV advertising,
    6–7, 48, 59
broadening the
    shoulders, 61–62
bumper stickers, 163
Burger King, 71
business card drawings,
    89–93, 211–212, 214
business card
    handshakes, 88–89
business immune system,
    111–112
business journals, 58–59

**C**

cable TV advertising, 7, 52–53

calls to action
    personal relationships
        and, 22
    as tracking devices,
        40–42, 58
CDMA (cable designated
    market area), 52
charity tie-ins, 200
church bulletins, 11
clean-slate marketing,
    19–20
communication methods
    direct mail. *See* direct
        mail
    email, 40–41, 176–178
    faxing, 178–179
    telephone, 172–176
    voice mail, 169–172
community appreciation
    events, 194–195, 196
competitors, customers
    of, 172–173
consumer research,
    43. *See also* target
        audiences
consumer shows, 17–18
Consumers' Choice
    Award, 54
content, 151–152

contests, 214
conventions, 17
conversion
    from business-card
        handshake pro-
        motions, 88
    defined, 23
    from direct mail, 134,
        137
    from employee incen-
        tive promotions,
        114
    ROI and, 31, 34–37
co-op advertising, 15–16,
    53–54
cooperative list sharing,
    201
coupons, 37–38, 40, 41,
    147–149
critical mass in
    marketing, 51–52
cross promotions. *See also*
    promotions
    examples of, 93–95
    geographic control in,
        96–98
    influence in, 96–98
    investment and, 95
    in the loop promo-
        tions, 103–105
    non-merchant part-
        ners in, 100–102
    partner leads for, 93
    price integrity and, 98
    relationship building
        and, 105–106
    reverse cross promo-
        tions, 99–100
    ROI and, 95–98
    seasonal promotions,
        102–103
    setting up, 98–99
CUME, 57–58
customer referral
    promotions, 115–117
customers. *See also* target
    audiences
    of competitors,
        172–173

consumer research, 43
    new, determining
        value of, 31–35
    regular customers,
        35–37

**D**
daily newspapers, 5–6
data capture, 214–217
data mining
    birth announcements,
        219
    from business card
        drawings, 89–93,
        211–212, 214
    capturing data,
        214–217
    of competition,
        218–219
    divorce records, 219
    grassroots mentality
        and, 219–220
    for ideal clients,
        212–214
databases, 91
decals, window, 163
designated market area
    (DMA), 52
developmental markets,
    76–77
differentiation, 141–144
digital marketing. *See*
    internet marketing
direct mail
    advantages of,
        141–144
    on birthdays, 132–133
    to business owners'
        homes, 136
    for customer relations,
        141
    endorsed mailings,
        145–146
    following up with,
        136–138
    to known buyers,
        135–136
    lumpy mail cam-
        paigns, 141–144

micro-targeting with,
    130–132
    opportunity and, 144
    to people moving in,
        133–135
    relevance of, 129
    timing of, 132–135
    tracking results of, 40
    using with other tac-
        tics, 138–140
discounts, 124
DMA (designated market
    area), 52
domain names, 42, 159–
    160, 175
Domino's Pizza, 64
drawings, 89–93, 211–212,
    214

**E**
electronic newsletters,
    177
email, 40–41, 176–178
employee incentive
    contests, 113–115
endorsed mailings,
    145–146
environment, sales and,
    125–127
events. *See* promotional
    events
exhibitions, 17
e-zines, 177

**F**
faxes, 178–179
financial planning
    seminars, 193
following up, 136–138
food tastings, 192
forced referrals, 130–132

**G**
geographic control, 96–98
Goodyear, 70
grassroots marketing. *See
    also* marketing
    brand strategy in, 4–5
    business cards in,
        88–90

data mining and. *See* data mining
defined, ix
direct mail in. *See* direct mail
events in. *See* promotional events
focus of, 69–70
local-level marketing in. *See* local-level marketing
mass media in. *See* mass advertising media
neighborhood marketing in, 67
No-B.S. Marketer traits, 25
non-traditional marketing, 11–12. *See also* websites
outdoor advertising in, 9–10, 24, 161–169
promotions in. *See* promotions
publicity in. *See* publicity
relationships in. *See* relationship building
seven-step marketing plan for, 75–81
tracking results of. *See* tracking results
traditional marketing, 5–11
truths about, 221–223
guerrilla marketing. *See* grassroots marketing

**H**
home-parties, 192–193
hurdle rate, 29

**I**
immune system, business, 111–112
inbound inquiries, 12–13, 62, 215

in-field execution, 77
inflatable displays, 168–169
influence, 96–98
in-office seminars, 192
internet marketing
links in, 156
online to offline follow-up, 137
sponsored links in, 149, 156–157
tools for, 11–12
updating, 160
web coupons in, 147–149
websites in. *See* websites
investment, 95–96

**K**
keywords, 152–154

**L**
links, 156
local business, 22–25, 109–112. *See also* local-level marketing
local marketing. *See* local-level marketing
local politics, 107–108
local store marketing (LSM). *See also* local-level marketing
common mistakes in, 75
defined, 67
ROI and, 33–36
local-level marketing. *See also* grassroots marketing
common mistakes in, 73–74
defined, 68–69
implementation of, 72–74
maintenance phase in, 84–85
marketing teams in, 85
neighborhood marketing, 67

plans in. *See* marketing plans
poor performance in, 83
reasons for, 70–71
relationship building in. *See* relationship building
revising materials for, 81–82
rollout process in, 82–83
training phase in, 77–81
logos, 15
lumpy mail, 141–144

**M**
macro ROI, 28–29
magnetic signs, 163
Market Development Funds (MDF), 53–54
market research, 43. *See also* target audiences
marketing. *See also* grassroots marketing
advertising. *See* advertising
critical mass in, 51–52
to customers of competitors, 172–174
effectiveness of, 1–4, 28–29, 75–76
logos in, 15
marketing plans. *See* marketing plans
media choices in, 24–25
ROI and. *See* return on investment (ROI)
selling function in, 13–14
situational aspect of, 24
vendors in, 15
zero-based, 19–20
marketing events. *See* promotional events

marketing plans
accountability in, 28
desired results of, 27
seven-step plan, 75–81
tracking results of. *See*
tracking results
marketing programs. *See*
marketing plans
mascots, 168
mass advertising media
on limited budget, 55
local-level marketing
and, 68
maximizing advertis-
ing dollars with,
50–54
negotiating price
with, 59–60
newspaper advertis-
ing. *See* newspa-
per advertising
radio advertising, 8–9,
55–58, 61
reaching critical mass,
51–52
shortcomings of, 47–48
TV advertising. *See*
TV advertising
Yellow Pages adver-
tising, 10–11,
62–64
McDonalds, 71
measuring results. *See*
tracking results
media choices, 24–25
merchant cross
promotions. *See* cross
promotions
messaging, 4–5
meta tags, 152
micro-targeting, 130–132
Moe's Southwest Grill,
93–94
monetizing websites, 160
Motel 6, 64–65
MP3 technology, 9
multi-input return on
investment (ROI),
33, 37

**N**
neighborhood blitzes, 124
neighborhood marketing,
67. *See also* grassroots
marketing; local-level
marketing
new neighbor events,
133–135
news outlets, 183–185
newspaper advertising
in daily newspapers,
5–6
sticky notes for, 53
in weekly/suburban
newspapers,
11, 58
No-B.S. Marketer traits, 25
nostalgia anchors, 126

**O**
object enclosed mail,
141–144
old customers, 35–37
online marketing. *See*
internet marketing
online to offline follow-
up, 137
outdoor advertising,
9–10, 24, 161–169
overnight advertising
spots, 55

**P**
parodies, 204–209
pay-per-click (PPC), 149,
156–157
penny savers, 11
phone numbers. *See*
telephone numbers
politics and business,
107–109
presentation materials,
81–82
press releases, 154
price integrity, 98
print advertising, 11.
*See also* newspaper
advertising
product-specific tracking
methods, 41–42

promotional codes, 40–41
promotional events. *See
also* promotions
attracting large num-
bers to, 200–204
charity tie-ins for, 200
for community appre-
ciation, 194–195,
196
consumer shows,
17–18
conventions, 17
creativity in, 197–198
for customer appre-
ciation, 194–195,
196
financial planning
seminars, 193
food tastings, 192
free, 199–200
home-parties, 192–193
locating, 197
in-office seminars, 192
parodies, 204–209
planning, 200
pre-registration for,
196
promoting, 195–197,
200–204
ROI of, 198–199
for selling one to
many, 191–192
speakers for, 199
speaking to sell and,
193–194
sponsorships for, 18–19
themes for, 197
wine-tastings, 192
promotions. *See also*
promotional events
appointments, reward
program for
keeping, 119–120
business card draw-
ings, 89–93
business card hand-
shakes, 88–89
cross promotions. *See*
cross promotions

customer referral programs, 115–117
dogs eat free, 123–124
employee incentive contests, 113–115
internal marketing, 122–123
neighborhood blitzes, 124
products for, 19
reciprocal displays, 121
redemptions, 37–38
suggest-sell contests, 117–119
worst seat in the house discount, 124
prospects. *See* target audiences
public relations, 182–185. *See also* publicity
publicity
directories, public relations, 184
firms, public relations, 182–183
generating, 185–187
handling negative, 187–189
leveraging, 185
local, 189
news outlets for, 183–185
pros and cons of, 16–17, 181–182
ROI of, 183

**Q**
quarter hour, 57–58

**R**
R3 group sessions, 78–80
radio advertising, 8–9, 55–58, 61
reciprocal displays, 121
redemptions, 37–38, 40
regular customers, 35–37
relationship building. *See also* local marketing

business card handshakes and, 88
business immune systems and, 111–112
conversion rates and, 134–135
in direct mail, 144–146
following up and, 137
knowing sellers personally, 22–25
one-on-one relationships in, 109–111
remnants, 61
return on investment (ROI). *See also* tracking results
accountability and, 28
calculating, 29–31
conversion rates and, 31, 34–37
cross promotions and, 95–98
of events, 198–199
local store marketing (LSM) and, 33–36. *See also* local-level marketing
marketing effectiveness and, 28–29
multi-input ROI, 33, 37
on promotions, 38
of publicity, 183
tracking devices and, 40–43
types of, 32–33
value of new customers in, 31–35
value of old customers in, 35–37
worthy ROI, 39–40
reward promotions, 119–120
rollout process, 82–83

**S**
sales
impact of environment on, 125–127

increasing on local level, 38–39
Sales Choreography, 126–127
Scarborough Research, 51
scattergrams, 90–91
school bulletins, 11
search engine optimization (SEO), 149–156
seasonal businesses, 61–62
seven-step marketing plan, 75–81. *See also* marketing plans
shock 'n' awe packages, 143–144
signature lines in email, 177–178
signs, 163–166
spectaculars, 168
sponsored links, 149, 156–157
SQAD, 52, 59
start anew marketing, 19–20
sticky notes, 53
submissions, 155
suburban newspapers, 11, 58
suggest-sell contests, 117–119
Super 8 Motels, 64
supervised in-field execution, 77

**T**
target audiences
consumer research and, 43
local media and, 48
micro-targeting, 130–132
prospect databases, 91
radio advertising and, 56–57
reaching, 47–48, 55–59, 96, 121
understanding, 50–51

telephone marketing,
12–13
telephone numbers
business names/ser-
vices in, 174
directory listings,
64–65
of former competitors,
172–173
memorable, 174–176
as tracking devices,
40–42
television advertising. *See*
TV advertising
testimonials, 21–22
*Think and Grow Rich*
(Hill), 25
tracking results. *See also*
return on investment
(ROI)
accountability and, 28
calls to action for,
40–42, 58
coupons for, 41
of direct mail, 40
email addresses for,
40–41
managing tracking
efforts, 43–44
promotional codes
for, 40–41
redemptions for,
37–38, 40
specific to product
tracking, 41–42

telephone numbers as,
40–42
untrackable market-
ing approaches,
44–45
value of, 46
worthy ROI and, 39–40
trade shows, 17
training, 77–81
TV advertising
on broadcast TV, 6–7,
48, 59
on cable TV, 7, 52–53
effectiveness of, 3
TV tags, 52–53

**U**

*Uncensored Sales Strategies*
(Barrows and
Kennedy), 126–127
Unique Selling
Propositions, 21
unit selection, 76–77
URLs, 42, 159–160, 175

**V**

vanity plates, 162
vehicle advertising,
161–164
voice mail, 169–172

**W**

wallscapes, 168
web coupons, 147–149
websites
content of, 151–152

costs of, 12
developing, 157–159
keywords in, 152–154
links in, 156
marketing, 159–160
meta tags in, 152
pay per click in, 149,
156–157
press releases and,
154
SEO for, 149–156
submissions and, 155
weekly newspapers,
11, 58
welcome gifts, 134
window decals, 163
wine-tastings, 192
Wizard of Sales parody,
The, 204–209
word of mouth, 125–127
worthy ROI, 39–40

**Y**

yard signs, 164–166
Yellow Pages advertising,
10–11, 62–64

**Z**

zero-based marketing,
19–20
zone spots, 52–53

# The Most Incredible
# <u>FREE</u> Gift Ever

## ($633.91 Worth of Pure Money-Making Information)

Dan Kennedy & Bill Glazer are offering an incredible opportunity for you to see WHY <u>Glazer-Kennedy Insider's Circle</u>™ is known as "<u>THE PLACE</u>" where <u>entrepreneurs seeking FAST and Dramatic Growth and greater Control, Independence, and Security come together</u>. Dan & Bill want to give you **$633.91 worth of pure Money-Making Information** including TWO months as an 'Elite' Gold Member of Glazer-Kennedy's Insider's Circle™. You'll receive a steady stream of MILLIONAIRE Maker Information including:

★ **Glazer-Kennedy University: Series of 3 Webinars (Value = $387.00)**

**The 10 BIG Breakthroughs in Business Life** *with "MILLIONARE Maker" Dan Kennedy*
* HOW <u>Any</u> Entrepreneur or Sales Professional can Multiply INCOME by 10X
* **HOW to Avoid Once and for All being an** *"Advertising Victim"*
* The "*<u>Hidden Goldmine</u>*" in Everyone's Business and HOW to Capitalize on it
* **The BIGGEST MISTAKE most Entrepreneurs make in their Marketing**
* And the <u>BIGGEEE</u>…Getting Customers Seeking You Out.

**The ESSENTIALS to Writing Million Dollar Ads & Sales Letters BOTH Online & Offline**
*with Bill Glazer*
* How to INCREASE the Selling Power of <u>All</u> Your Advertising with the <u>13 "Must Have" Direct Response Principles</u>
* **Key Elements that Determine the Success of Your Website**
* How to Craft a Headline the Grabs the Reader's Attention
* **HOW to Create an Irresistible Offer that Melts Away <u>Any</u> Resistance to Buy**
* The <u>Best</u> Ways to Create Urgency and Inspire IMMEDIATE Response
* **"*Insider Strategies*" to INCREASE Response that you <u>Must</u> be using both ONLINE & Offline**

**The ESSENTIALS of Productivity & Implementation for Entrepreneurs**
*with Peak Performance Coach Lee Milteer*
* How to Almost INSTANTLY be MORE Effective, Creative, Profitable, and Take MORE Time Off
* **HOW to Master the "Inner Game" of Personal Peak Productivity**
* How to Get MORE Done in Less Time
* **HOW to Get Others to Work On <u>Your</u> Schedule**
* How to Create Clear Goals for SUCESSFUL Implementation
* **And Finally the <u>BIGGEE</u>…HOW to Stop Talking and Planning Your Dreams and Start Implementing them into Reality**

★ **'Elite' Gold Insider's Circle Membership (Two Months Value = $119.94):**

* TWO Issues of *The NO B.S. Marketing Letter:*

Each issue is at least 24 pages – usually MORE – Overflowing with **the latest Marketing & Money-Making Strategies**. Current members refer to it as <u>a day-long intense seminar in print</u>, arriving by first class mail every month. There are ALWAYS terrific examples of *"What's-Working-NOW"* **Strategies**, timely Marketing news, trends, ongoing teaching of <u>Dan Kennedy's Most IMPORTANT Strategies</u>… and MORE. As soon as it arrives in your mailbox you'll want to find a quiet place, grab a highlighter, and devour every word.

- Two CDs Of The **EXCLUSIVE GOLD AUDIO INTERVIEWS**

  EXCLUSIVE interviews with successful users of direct response advertising, leading experts and entrepreneurs in direct marketing, and famous business authors and speakers. Use them to turn commuting hours into **"POWER Thinking" Hours.**

★ **The New Member No B.S. Income Explosion Guide & CD** (Value = $29.97)

  This resource is especially designed for NEW MEMBERS to show them HOW they can join the thousands of Established Members **creating exciting sales and PROFIT growth** in their Business, Practices, or Sales Careers & Greater SUCCESS in their Business lives.

★ **Income Explosion FAST START Tele-Seminar with Dan Kennedy, Bill Glazer, and Lee Milteer** (Value = $97.00)

  Attend from the privacy and comfort of your home or office...hear a DYNAMIC discussion of Key Advertising, Marketing, Promotion, Entrepreneurial & Phenomenon strategies, PLUS answers to the most Frequently Asked Questions about these Strategies

★ **You'll also get these Exclusive "Members Only" Perks:**

  - **Special FREE Gold Member CALL-IN TIMES:** Several times a year, Dan & I schedule Gold-Member ONLY Call-In times.
  - **Gold Member RESTRICTED ACCESS WEBSITE**: Past issues of the *NO B.S. Marketing Letter*, articles, special news, etc.
  - **Continually Updated MILLION DOLLAR RESOURCE DIRECTORY** with Contacts and Resources Dan & his clients use.

*There is a one-time charge of $19.95 in North America or $39.95 International to cover postage. After your 2-Month FREE test-drive, you will automatically continue at the lowest Gold Member price of $59.97 per month. Should you decide to cancel your membership, you can do so at any time by calling Glazer-Kennedy Insider's Circle™ at 410-825-8600 or faxing a cancellation note to 410-825-3301 (Monday through Friday 9am – 5pm). Remember, your credit card will NOT be charged the low monthly membership fee until the beginning of the third month, which means you will receive 2 full issues to read, test, and **profit from all of the powerful techniques and strategies you get from being an Insider's Circle Gold Member.** And of course, it's impossible for you to lose, because if you don't absolutely LOVE everything you get, you can simply cancel your membership after the second free issue and never get billed a single penny for membership.

------------------------------------------------------------

**\*EMAIL REQUIRED IN ORDER TO NOTIFY YOU ABOUT THE GLAZER-KENNEDY UNIVERSITY WEBINARS AND FAST START TELESEMINAR\***

Name _____ Business Name _____

Address _____

City _____ State _____ Postal Code _____ Country _____

Phone _____ Fax _____

E-mail* _____

Credit Card Instructions to Cover $19.95 Postage ($39.95 International)

Credit Card: ____Visa ____MasterCard ____ American Express ____ Discover

Credit Card Number _____ Exp. Date _____

Signature _____ Date _____

Providing this information constitutes your permission for Glazer-Kennedy Insider's Circle™ to contact you regarding related information via mail, e-mail, fax, and phone.

**FAX BACK TO 410-825-3301**
**Or mail to: 401 Jefferson Ave., Towson, MD 21286**
**www.dankennedy.com**